Success Reframe

6 Steps to 6 Figures in Superman Tights

Shirley Billson

Copyright © August 2013 Shirley Billson

All rights reserved.

www.shirleybillson.com The views expressed in this work are solely those of the author and do not necessarily reflect the views of the publisher, and the publisher hereby disclaims any responsibility for them.

The author of this book does not dispense financial or medical advice or prescribe the use of any technique as a form of treatment for physical, emotional, medical or financial problems without the advice of a physician or financial professional, either directly or indirectly. The intent of the author is only to offer information of a general nature to help you in your quest for emotional and spiritual well-being. In the event you use any of the information in this book for yourself, which is your constitutional right, the author and the publisher assumes no responsibility for your actions.

Dedication and acknowledgements

I'd like to acknowledge the unwavering faith of my partner, Lewis, who has supported me through every up and every down of this rollercoaster ride I call my business. He has never doubted me even when I have doubted myself. He has trusted my judgement, my intent and my ability at every moment – even through his own low moments - and, without him, I may well have given up long ago. He is a man of unwavering strength and humility – and, though I tell him often, he still doesn't know it.

I'd also like to thank my son, Robert, who is a source of pride to me in every waking moment. From the moment he was born, I fell in love and never fail to be inspired by his nature and his spirit. Sometimes, to his personal cost, I have forgotten moments when he needed to just be a child and yet, whatever he has thought privately, he has only ever openly loved and supported me and cheered me on from the side-lines. He encourages me in ways that he may not even realise. I am truly a better person because of him and I thank him from the bottom of my heart.

I am also blessed.by step children, Scott and Elliott, who have always been a joy to spend time with – and have unselfishly shared their father's love with me. I do not underestimate how fortunate that makes me.

I'd like to thank the clients past and present, who have allowed me to share some of their stories in the pages of this book. I know that the stories of their journeys will be the impetus for many of you to begin your own.

Then there's the clients who have become friends, and the many dear friends I have met through my own coach's extended community. They have taught me to not fear vulnerability and have supported and held me aloft when I have felt weak and wanted to crumble.

I have witnessed their low moments too – and they have helped me see that it is not only possible, but desirable, to be a deeply caring and committed human being, and combine financial with spiritual wealth.

Each one of those people, too many to mention, has touched me and given me more than they realise.

Finally, I'd like to thank my coach, Kendall Summerhawk and her wonderful family, who have each taught me so much, practically and emotionally. Many of the practical sections within this book around niche, charging and signature systems are hers and I reproduce them here with full permission as a CMMS (Certified Money, Marketing and Soul®) coach.

Contents

SUCCESS REFRAME	1
FOREWORD	9
CHAPTER ONE: THE PRE-FRAME - GREAT EXPECTATIONS	10
You can do this!	11
Hobby or business? My story	12
Satisfying an ambition	14
Projected income seems good	15
Creating a legacy of power	18
CHAPTER TWO: REFRAME 1 - 'FEAR OF 'MAKING IT'	22
Change and the battle for survival	23
Fear of doing things differently	24
Who says you can't?	25
The influence of environment	26
Difficult conversations	27
First time fears	31
Fear of being visible and standing out	32
Money and risk	33
Work life balance	35
Physician, heal thyself	36
CHAPTER THREE: REFRAME 2 - MONEY	40
Charging by the hour	40
It's not about the money	42
It's greedy to charge more	45
It's wrong to love money	46
Charging more means exploiting and excluding people who 'can't afford it	47
CHAPTER FOUR: REFRAME 3 - POSSIBILITY	50
You are an expert	51
Vision, Passion and Purpose	53
Lifting the veil on the blind-spot	57
Express your needs and desires	58
Where to begin	59
CHAPTER FIVE: REFRAME 4 – BEING GOOD ENOUGH	63

BRAG WITH STYLE 65
GET POWERFUL TESTIMONIALS 68
TAKE CREDIT WHERE IT'S DUE 72
AN OUNCE OF PRE-FRAMING IS WORTH A POUND OF REFRAMING 75
CREATE A VISION FOR SUCCESS – WITH TIMELINES AND GOALS THAT EXCITE YOU. 79
EXERCISE: HOW TO QUICKLY CREATE A HIGH END STATE OF MIND (SUMMERHAWK) 81

CHAPTER SIX: REFRAME 5 – EXPERT STATUS 84

HERE'S THE GOOD NEWS. BEING AN EXPERT DOESN'T MEAN YOU NEED TO 84
WHAT COUNTS AS EXPERT KNOWLEDGE? 84
HOW TO CONVERT EXPERT KNOWLEDGE TO EXPERT STATUS WITH EASE 85

CHAPTER SEVEN: REFRAME 6 - NICHE MATTERS 89

OVERCOME RESISTANCE 91
LUCRATIVE NICHE ADVANTAGE 93
LOVE YOUR CLIENTS 95
7 STEPS TO A LUCRATIVE NICHE 95
Step one: Re-define the business you're in 95
Step two: Choose a category 98
Step three: Identify potential groups 99
Step four: Identify what problems you are solving 102
Step five: Choose your ideal niche 105
Step six: Identify the tribe within the niche 107
Step seven: Make your final choice 111

CHAPTER EIGHT: REFRAME 7 - CORE MARKETING STRATEGIES 113

MEANINGFUL MARKETING 113
AVOID 'BUFFET' MARKETING 114
GETTING CLEAR ON YOUR DREAM CLIENT 116
MARKETING WITHIN A NICHE 117
USP (UNIQUE SELLING POINT) 118
YOUR INTRODUCTORY MARKETING MESSAGE (THE ELEVATOR PITCH) 120
RETURN ON PROMOTIONAL INVESTMENT. 122
DISCOUNT PRICING STRATEGIES 124
GOAL SETTING 126
MEASURABLE ACTIONS 127

SIMPLE 7-STEP CLIENT ATTRACTING SYSTEM	129
LIST BUILDING AND OPT-INS	130
DOWNLOADABLE FREE GIFT	132
ENROLMENT CONVERSATIONS	132
SIGNATURE TALK	133
DECISION MAKING	134
CASE STUDY	137
CHAPTER NINE: REFRAME 8 - CHARGING	**140**
WHAT HOTELS CAN TEACH YOU	142
PREMIUM PRICING	144
Most people associate quality with price	*144*
Case study: The coffee shop lesson	*146*
THE VALUE OF GIVING PEOPLE WHAT THEY REALLY WANT	148
WORKING WITH YOU IS AN INVESTMENT, NOT A COST	150
Example: A sloooow learner	*152*
MANAGING RESISTANCE	155
EXERCISE: THE VALUE OF WORKING WITH YOU	157
The cost of not working with you	*157*
CHARGING WHAT YOU'RE WORTH ATTRACTS MORE OF YOUR DREAM CLIENTS	157
OPEN THE DOOR TO BIGGER INCOME OPPORTUNITIES	159
ATTRACT HIGH END CLIENTS WITH HIGH END PROGRAMMES	160
WHO IS A HIGH END CLIENT?	161
WHAT IS A HIGH END PROGRAMME?	162
EXERCISE: CREATING A PROGRAMME	163
EXERCISE: CAPTURE YOUR SIGNATURE SYSTEM	165
Example: My 5-step signature system:	*166*
HOW TO GO FROM 'WHAT IS A HIGH END PROGRAMME?' TO OFFERING ONE	167
HOW TO CREATE YOUR OWN HIGH END PROGRAMME	168
High End Programme Sample Blueprint	*172*
Sample High End Success Plan	*173*
CHAPTER TEN: REFRAME 9 – PRESENT STATE OF MIND	**176**
CONSIDERING A COACH AND MENTOR	177
SUCCESS REFRAME PRIVATE PROGRAMMES, MASTERMIND GROUPS AND WORKSHOPS	179
ABOUT THE AUTHOR	**180**
THE LAST WORD.	182

BIBLIOGRAPHY 184

Foreword

I qualified as a Solutions Focused Hypnotherapist in 2006 and was told to set my fees at £55 per hour. The last time I charged anyone by the hour was in 2012 and I had increased my fees to £90 for half an hour. Apart from a handful of Harley Street Hypnotherapists, I was charging way above the norm.

By the time I changed the whole structure of my business and stopped charging by the hour, I was horrified to discover that newly qualified hypnotherapy graduates – and experienced hypnotherapists alike - were charging the same or less than when I had qualified 6 years prior.

I saw many who were either struggling to make a full time business; or trading overwhelm for 'success.'

Whatever 'evidence' you are using to convince yourself that you have no choice in this, I hope that by the time you finish this book, you will see that it is possible to choose the hours you work, the clients you work with and the money you make.

Chapter One:
The Pre-frame - Great Expectations

This book is for you if you are achieving some success and want to step up to another level, but have so many creative ideas for expansion that it is hard to keep track of them or follow any through to completion without being sidetracked by more.

This book is for you if you are achieving considerable success, but feel too overwhelmed to fully implement all of the ideas you have for sustainable growth.

This book is for you if you are not achieving the success you want – and that you know is possible – if you could only get some help with the key steps.

This book may challenge your perceptions of what you believe is possible. It will challenge you to think about your business differently, to think about money differently and to think about yourself differently.

This book is not a magic pill; but it does lift the lid on marketing and business building practices that work equally well for the hypnotherapist entrepreneur, the healer, or the coach, who wants to build a business based on integrity and authenticity.

You are about to benefit from the tens of thousands of pounds I have invested in seeking out answers, from my mistakes and my successes, my heartbreak and my celebration.

I was a disillusioned business woman and marketing specialist out of integrity with myself. In 2006, I became a hypnotherapist and thought I had discovered nirvana.

In the seven years that followed, I had to re-evaluate everything I thought I knew about myself, business, money, marketing and hypnotherapy.

I have come full circle to rediscover myself as a gifted hypnotherapist and mentor with marketing expertise, uniquely placed to support others to achieve their own dreams of success, without compromising their ideals.

I'd like you to join me on a journey to meet the bigger, bolder, richer version of you and your business.

You can do this!

In the pages of the book, I share each of the step by step 'how to' processes I share with my private clients. I also explode many of the myths that might be presenting stumbling blocks to your belief that you can succeed at creating a financially successful and spiritually rewarding business.

I want you to remember on every page that you can do this. You do not have to be someone different, someone in a different life, someone with more luck, someone with more expertise. You just have to be you.

Think of your own clients for a moment – or, if you are completely new – think of your prospective clients.

You hold them as powerful and capable of the change they doubt. You help them see new possibility, let go of the fear that holds them back and you believe in them when they don't believe in themselves.

Even though they may say they have become a new person, you know they have simply become more of the person who was already there, freed from doubt and anxiety, liberated to explore their ambitions and dreams – even if it is only to walk to the end of the road without checking 28 times that the front door is locked.

You make more possible, by simply opening a door for your clients to step through...a door into a space where they can find themselves, discover they are powerful, and make astonishing change.

I am opening just such a door for you in the pages of this book.

Whatever your background, your education, your level of success, or the 'reality' you currently hold, more is possible for you. Much more. You just have to be willing to step in and commit to take action with an open mind.

Remember, if the answer to what you seek (greater success, financial stability, freedom, ease) were in your current version of what you believe is possible for you, you would have achieved it by now.

The lack of it says you need help – to reframe your sense of what is possible, to move past fear and doubt, scatter and overwhelm - and to create the life and business that is possible for you. It starts here. It starts today.

The belief I hold for you on every page is this:

You are powerful. You are extraordinary. You are capable.

Welcome.

HOBBY OR BUSINESS? MY STORY

Some of you might wonder if what you chose to do as a living has become more of a hobby. Sometimes, even the people closest to you might say as much.

Perhaps you are busy seeing lots of clients and feeling great about it; if only you could free up some time to consistently channel some of the many creative ideas you have for expanding your business.

Maybe you have a habit of enthusiastically diving into an exciting new project but never quite completing it before another one catches your attention – and off you go again (bright shiny syndrome).

I have been in each of the above categories at one time or another.

I have struggled to make ends meet….and though feedback from clients was great, praise and a warm glow weren't currency I could pay my bills with.

There was one year I made a figure just shy of £50,000…and I thought I had on the verge of having cracked it.

Then I spent a lot of time and energy trying to figure out how to capitalise on that success and create passive income, so that I could relax and enjoy the success I was having, plus have a retirement to look forward to.

I created my own online programme for people with eating disorders, after I appeared on TV in a documentary on the subject. It was called Ditch the Binge and those who signed up for it loved it, but it wasn't the 'sit on the beach and count the money' kind of passive income the internet marketers promised.

I thought that niche was the way to go. It was, but I didn't have all the pieces of the jigsaw I needed to make it a success back then.

It was a lot of work at my desk for not a lot of income.

I updated my web site (often), wrote articles and blogs, created leaflets and business cards, joined networking groups, spoke at workshops and conferences (some paid, some free), made videos and audios, signed up for internet marketing programmes, free webinars and every kind of free download you can imagine.

I had been unwittingly sucked into the belief that online was the answer – and that, as long as I could get high enough in the search engines using clever tools and techniques, I would get the traffic that would bring me the business and the income – for a very low investment. Not true.

I was doing lots of the right things, but it was bit like having all the ingredients for a recipe but no idea what the right amounts were or when they should be added.

Fortunately, my experience – that involved a lot of mistakes, a lot of money and a lot of tears - has, thankfully, led me to the place where I can now write this book.

In my very first year of adopting a fresh business model and a fresh perspective on what was possible – the model I lay out for you here – I achieved my first 5 figure month EVER.

I share my entire system with you in the pages that follow.

SATISFYING AN AMBITION

We are all motivated differently, but we all have ambition – even if our dashed dreams force us to deny it, even to ourselves.

The ambition, perhaps, is to be your own boss, without the need to follow someone else's rules, or to make enough money to change your own or your family's lives, or to help change the world, to do work with meaning, to feel like you are really contributing to life and the universe, or to feel fulfilled and rewarded with the joy of seeing the transformations YOU got to play a part in creating - and to get paid for doing it.

Or, perhaps, you see the potential for building a real business, perhaps with a grand plan that includes authorship, workshops, a lucrative niche, corporate clients - or maybe forays into the online space with an online shop and hypnosis mp3s, cds or iPhone apps.

SOMETHING TO PROVE

Maybe you always dreamed of working for yourself and wanted to prove – to yourself or to others – that you could do this; that you could step off of the corporate treadmill; or pick yourself up after redundancy, or child-rearing, or sickness, or simply step out from someone else's shadow – and transform yourself, your life and your income in one fulfilling monumental step.

LEAVING CORPORATE STRESS BEHIND

The prospect of answering to no-one or working from home may have lured you. Maybe you thought it would be pressure free. Perhaps you thought you had traded the stresses and worries of 'ordinary' working life for this new career as a fully qualified hypnotherapist.

PROJECTED INCOME SEEMS GOOD

At the outset, it all looked great. You worked out the hourly rate, figured in a reasonable number of client hours per week – and thought that would do nicely.

Perhaps you factored in that it would evolve with time…so you didn't worry if it grew slowly to begin with…and you didn't invest 'too much'. You might have convinced yourself that slow growth was the sensible, safe way to go, meaning low investment but steady gains.

The sad facts are that this work you love can, indeed, begin to look a lot like a hobby. The costs of advertising to get more clients, paying clinic session fees, investing in more and more CPD and additional qualifications (in an effort to get more clients), almost outweigh the income you get from the unpredictable drift of weekly clients.

Even if you are earning what you think is great money, the moment you stop so does the money.

It's frustrating, because when you do the maths at the beginning, it all looks so easy. A healthy hourly rate and no more than 10 to 15 clients per week seems reasonable.

Whatever your old job used to pay, the projected income could provide a healthy contribution to household bills – which would mean you could hold your head up high; have enough money to live on and enough time to enjoy it.

The trouble is, however good you are, you are dependent on how many hourly paid clients turn up each week; and how healthy and fit you remain.

And that is unpredictable. Scarily unpredictable.

There's an absolute ceiling on your income when you work to the hourly paid practice model, with no effective provision for sickness, time out, or effective retirement planning.

Even when you are successful, unless you have a master plan for how to generate income when the clients stop, the profession is not setting you up for future financial success and security.

Once you factor in no-shows and late cancellations, what started out looking like a good week can end up with a handful of clients drifting in at opposite ends of a day, with you re-organising your notes and preparing for more clients who don't turn up - or spending more on coffee and snacks in the breaks between.

You either aren't earning enough – or you are in fear of not earning enough – and the stress is in danger of leaking into your client work; making it less successful, less satisfying and creating the downward spiral of anxiety you know all too well because you explain it often to your clients.

Or, you are so busy seeing clients and travelling between clinics that you can't find the time to build the passive income that will give you more freedom, even though you are brimming with ideas to make that happen.

This was the position I found myself in.

I was seeing around 10 – 15 clients per week in 3 clinics, one of which was an hour's drive away and I was responsible for the lease on the building too.

I didn't live in a big house, I didn't have lots of assets and I didn't have any pension provision…so, for me, it was never going to be enough.

When I was seeing enough clients, I didn't have time to focus on building other income streams, and when I wasn't seeing enough clients, I didn't believe I had the finances to 'risk' and make other options possible for me.

Eventually, on my 50th birthday, I reached a point where I would rather risk failing than end my days wondering why I hadn't made it when, deep down, I knew I was capable of more.

There's something about turning 50 that makes thoughts turn to replaying the first half of your life and imagining the final outcome of the second half!

Dying with a little more debt, but knowing I had given it my best shot seemed infinitely preferable to wondering what might have been.

I wasn't married to someone well off, had no savings or comfortable divorce settlement. I had nothing to look forward to in retirement unless I could create it for myself; and I had to do it now, while there was still time to achieve it – and enjoy it.

I finally made a big, scary decision about my business – and took full responsibility for creating something awesome, something that really expressed me and what I was capable of – and something that supported me (rather than me – or someone else - supporting it).

I had to make more and create something bigger – and I was driven to find out how; not just for myself, but for the legacy I was creating for my son.

I just couldn't remain in integrity with myself or him if I urged him to follow his dreams, to believe that anything was possible if only he stayed focussed and committed – if I didn't act on that assertion myself.

CREATING A LEGACY OF POWER

Do you ever want more for your children, for your partner, for friends?

Do you ever get frustrated when you witness those closest to you overlooking or underestimating their own talents and failing to follow their dreams for lack of confidence or fear of failure?

Do you ever get overwhelmed with so many ideas that never come to fruition because you just can't figure out what to do first – or you chase down lots of avenues, never quite reaching it to the end before something new and exciting takes you off down another path?

We cannot change others; we can only change ourselves; but in changing ourselves, we create the possibility that people around us will change too. Every one of us has the potential to create possibility for others, whether we do it knowingly or not.

I firmly believe the following:

➢ We are the architects and creators of our own experience.

➢ the creation of that experience depends on what we believe

➢ what we believe is largely influenced by the role models in our lives and what they do

➢ what we do or don't do lays down subconscious patterns for future generations

We cannot tell them what to do or who to be, but, in my opinion, if you truly want your children to follow a path of expansion and possibility, of focus and implementation, you will have a better chance of that being the case if you are prepared to practise what you preach – and model it for them.

My own path to success was paved by a desire for my son to see his brilliance, to believe that he was good enough to do anything, be anybody and go anywhere. Like most parents, I wanted him to be happy and free, the master of his own destiny.

However, the older he got, the more hollow my sentiments seemed.

As I witnessed his own self-doubt and wavering confidence with frustration, I realised it was no good me remonstrating with him, advising him to trust his intuition, to focus on what he wanted and to take action on achieving it.

I would have to confront my own fears, my own self-doubt and go out and prove that what I was saying was true.

Of course, I cannot determine what he chooses or whether he follows my path or another – but I can be confident that I have done everything in my power to model *what is possible.*

Exercise: The real cost of getting a client

There are all kinds of ways of learning from your figures – and, if you are serious about your 'business' and intent that this is NOT A HOBBY, you need to get familiar with them. You must understand what they reveal and allow that to feed into your decision making.

Most hypnotherapists have NO IDEA what their returns on investment are or even what their numbers are, so here's a simple way you can start to get familiar with that:

1. *Add up how many clients you have seen in the past year (not the number of client hours, but the number of clients).*

2. *Add up ALL your costs (advertising, CPD, supervision, training, clinic costs) If you work from home, don't assume this is cost free – factor in heating, lighting, phone, etc.*

3. *Add up your total client income.*

Divide the answer to 2 by the answer to 1.

This is the average cost of getting a client.

Say the amount spent on costs was £10,000 and the number of clients was 50. This means the average cost of getting a client is: £10,000/50=£200

Now divide the answer to 3 by the answer to 1.

This is the average revenue generated by a client.

Say the total income generated was £12,500. This means the average revenue generated by a client is: £12,500/50=£250

If you only look at the total costs and the total revenue, you might panic, decide this IS proving to be 'just a hobby' and start frantically looking for jobs – or spend even more money trying to get more clients.

However, truly examining the detail in the figures reveals that there are other options:

If, for example, you were able to see each client, on average, for more sessions, the costs would stay the same, the number of clients would stay the same, but the income would increase. And, how often do clients actually benefit from more sessions?

The thing is, this kind of work also asks you to confront your own belief systems and personal challenges around money – and around client relationships; like feeling confident and powerful enough to advise a client, who needs more, to commit to more (without assuming they can't afford it, they won't like you, blah, blah).

The question is, do you want a fulfilling, successful business, built on reputation and trust – that enhances your own personal development on the way - or do you want an expensive hobby?

Chapter Two:
Reframe 1 - 'Fear of 'Making It'

There are two stages where fear kicks in:

The first stage is chronic and persistent. It can embody the fear of failing, of not making enough money, of creating more debt, all of those and some more besides.

These fears we recognise and they can provide the impetus to seek help through business coaching, marketing support - or some other form of learning.

It may be what drove you to read this book.

The second stage of fear comes not long after and it can take you by surprise.

I've experienced it myself – and I witness it in others.

Here's what happens:

What starts out as excitement – the desire to build a successful business, to have a higher income, to work only with dream clients – quickly and unexpectedly gives way to fear when presented with the solution.

It tends to shift from 'chronic and persistent' fear to sporadic but acute.

Fear can be wily and it might not even seem to be expressed as fear. More likely, we go into 'story' that starts with some of the following well used phrases:

"I can't do that, I have no time, I'm not good enough, I don't know enough, I can't do it yet, I'll do it later, my partner won't let me (invest), I don't have any money, I have too many other commitments, people won't like me"....and so on.

Maybe it's because we are so good at dealing with other people's fears that we don't feel comfortable seeking help for our own.

And maybe, despite the codes of ethics and professional confidence, seeking help from another hypnotherapist, about the success or otherwise of your business, can seem incongruous – especially when you know that many of them are struggling themselves.

So we struggle on. Hope, prayer, Google, SEO and denial become the business strategies of choice for many.

A very rare few invest in a high end business coach who's trodden the path before, who will guide you through the dark days, keep urging you on when you want to give up – and keep you focused on every success, preventing you from diminishing your own contribution, ability or gifts in any way.

CHANGE AND THE BATTLE FOR SURVIVAL

The amygdala is the primitive part of your brain responsible for survival. We all have individual, complex, subconscious patterns that trigger it to respond to different kinds of threat. Yet, there is one kind of fear that plays subtly in the background of our lives the whole time: change.

Beware the resistance, the procrastination, the doubt….it is triggered by your amygdala…which interprets the steps you are taking to make big changes as one's it needs to prevent. It wants you to play safe, to stay where you are. It perceives risk and it wants you to stop moving forward.

This is one time where you need to listen to what you really want and keep moving. Just like the title of the book, 'Feel the fear and do it anyway.' (Jeffers, 1987)

FEAR OF DOING THINGS DIFFERENTLY

I see this all the time. I'll be speaking at an event and I'll ask, "How many people are already making 6 figures in their business?"

Somewhere between zero and a handful put up their hands.

Then I ask, "How many would like to be making 6 figures in their business?"

Most hands go up.

Yet, what starts off as excitement and desire can quickly turn to fear and anxiety when you realise that you have to do things differently and think differently - and the cosy ways of working and marketing that our training schools taught us are not enough; not enough to create a sustainable, financially rewarding business with passive income flows, stable income and free time, that is.

Here's the bad news:

➢ You HAVE TO step out of your comfort zones.

➢ You HAVE to work on your own self development.

➢ You have to treat your practice as a business.

Here's the good news:

➢ None of this is beyond the skill or expertise of ANYONE reading this book.

Sadly, many of you will put the book down and never act on any of the desires that brought you to read it.

You will - like the clients you see in your own consulting room, who won't commit - stay stuck, stay under-fulfilled, stay underpaid or overwhelmed, stay wondering, "Could I....?"

Who says you can't?

You may have great intent to do things differently – but if you don't act quickly, you may end up staying exactly where you are and changing nothing.

When you hear yourself saying or thinking things like, "I can't...find the time, be that successful, make that call, do it that way, charge that much, earn that much", stop for a second and ask yourself where that voice of doubt or objection comes from.

Is it really yours? Or did someone, or something, along the way convince you that you couldn't – or that 'people like you' or 'people like us' couldn't.

In my experience, if there is an inner conflict, an inner dialogue that pulls in two different directions – the conflict comes from outside, from something that someone else believed or believes, and that you have, at some point, internalised and interpreted as your own. Or, you feel you *should* internalise as your own.

Again, think about how you respond to hearing your own clients voice such concerns about their own challenges...and notice how you can spot the dissonance.

Call it intuition, gut instinct, or acute observation – but you do notice the difference in tone and body language when a client expresses something that comes from their own heartfelt desires and beliefs – and something they have accepted as normal from outside; but which doesn't sit comfortably with them.

Observe it now in yourself. Reflect on it. Take this opportunity to change it.

The Influence of Environment

Your environment (and that includes the people in it) is critical to what you believe is possible for you – and what actions you take. It can propel you forward and empower you to step into a big place; or it can hold you back and keep you playing small.

Many psychological studies have shown this...yet, as individuals, we can sometimes feel like we are immune to it, masters of our own destiny and not swayed by the opinions of others to alter the course of our life away from what we might truly want or what is possible for us.

However, none of us are immune to the opinions and beliefs of our family and friends, our colleagues, the things we read or, sadly, the online social networks we spend (too much!) time in.

One of the most powerful shifts for change can come from your environment – and, yet it will be the one where you may experience greatest resistance.

If you are aware there are people in your life who hold you back – whose very company can set you back several steps from where you are every time you speak to them – you already know that something has to change.

It's just a case of when and how.

You might postpone it and procrastinate, but at some point, if you are serious about creating the fulfilling and successful business you want...you will have to do something about it.

Difficult Conversations

People who love you mean well – but their words and actions can actually do the very opposite of what's intended.

They want you to be safe, they want you to be happy….but, unwittingly, their advice and good intentions are fed by their own fears and doubts of what is possible for THEM; and they can project that onto you.

They may tell you how bad the economy is – and that there is no shame in 'failing;' they may tell you the market is tough for everyone and lots of people are going out of business; or that no-one has any money to spend; or that no-one would pay what you are asking; or that now is not the right time; or that you should get a job to be safe and only invest in your business when you have 'proved' that it will work.

They may play on your sense of guilt, your sense of deservability. You may fear disapproval, withdrawal of affection or love – and their expressions of doubt or fear feed your inner critics desire to stay right where you are.

And it isn't just friends or family – it's casual acquaintances, people you meet at work, fuelled by stories you read in the press or see on the news.

It builds a wall of objection, creates the sense of a huge mountain to climb; and though it is well disguised as good intent and rationality, it is really fed by your brain doing what it does best….looking for patterns that support your own limiting beliefs and finding them.

The first action you may need to take is not the first one you might choose to take – and it is astonishing the lengths some of us will go to, in order to avoid that first action.

The action? An honest conversation and an expression of our heartfelt needs and desires – without acrimony, without anger, without blame.

You need to calmly explain to those people what your intent is, that you would highly value their support and positivity – and that, if they are unwilling or unable to give that, you would prefer not to discuss it.

Some will respect that and come on board – because they truly do love you and want the best for you. Some, sadly, will not, which can result in tough choices to distance yourself from certain friends, colleagues or family.

It will not serve you well, or them, if you fail to act on what you know is right for you in your heart. A light will go out and your diminishment will impact on all those around you.

This is where you need to firmly consider what you truly want for YOU in your life; what will enable you to feel fulfilled and validated in living your life purpose; what legacy you want to create in this lifetime.

Instead, so many of us choose one of only two options:

1. carry on regardless (always wrong)

2. leave (sometimes wrong).

My own path through life was generally the latter of the two options. If the going got tough, I changed jobs, changed homes, changed friends, changed partners.

I convinced myself I was making positive changes to my life when what I was really doing was avoiding grown up conversations that could have changed the situation for the better.

In truth, I was running from myself – and repeatedly surprised when the same problems recurred wherever I went!

However much we might want it to be so, however much we try, it really is not possible to compartmentalise business and life and expect to hold it all together successfully for any sustained period.

Case study

Let me share with you the story of how this played out for a talented, intelligent and outwardly independent woman in her late 20's, who wanted to pursue her dream of entrepreneurship and creative freedom.

Her parents, wanting the best for her, 'expected' her to remain in the safe, respectable, profession of accountancy in a well-paying corporation. From their perspective, we might assume, she was very fortunate to have such blessings, when what they saw and read about in the news was young people saddled with debt, living at home and jobless.

She didn't feel able 'let them down' by sharing what her real passions in life were. Instead, she moved to the other side of the world (literally) to pursue her passion.

She found physical removal was easier than actually having a conversation with them about what she really wanted for herself in her life; and she thought, by doing so, she had solved the problem.

However, because she was still hiding out from the conversation that needed to happen (they thought she had moved as part of her job – and when they visited, she dressed up in a suit and went to sit in a library all day!), the success she wanted in following her passion continued to elude her.

The truth was that her inner critic began to do the job of parenting in their absence – and the logical part of her began to entertain the notion that they were right, even though her heart was telling her otherwise.

Her reluctance to trust what she wanted and what felt right for her when it came to conversations with her parents – was showing up in her conversations with prospective clients.

Self-doubt was like a badge tattooed on her forehead and it meant she was standing in the way of the success she desperately wanted and needed.

It was only when she was able to step into a place of adult power – to calmly state what it was that she wanted; to ask for respect in her decision, if not support - that she finally became free and was able to start enjoying the success she had always been so capable of – yet hadn't previously had the courage to step into.

So, when it comes to changing environment, sometimes it is the difficult conversations that are the biggest part of making that transition.

Only YOU can know that. Only you can decide.

However, I urge you to not hide from the unique brilliance of who you are, what is possible for you, and the gifts you bring to the world that are worthy of sharing as widely as possible.

I urge you to take the bold steps that bring you to the place of possibility, of potential, of fulfilment; to create abundance for yourself and others in the full sharing and expression of your abundant gifts.

In short, I urge you to love yourself rich.

First time fears

Remember how you learned to drive (or ski, or ride a bike, or some other new skill) and it was such a heavy mental process to begin with?

It was tricky to concentrate on all the things you had to do and manage co-ordination at the same time. Maybe you doubted you would ever 'get it'.

However, it is likely that the 'evidence' of people around you reassured you that it was very possible because 'everyone' was doing it. So you persisted until you succeeded.

When it came to learning hypnotherapy, you took the decision to do something different.

Even though you may have felt nervous and scared before your first practice session and your first client, with the support of class mates, supervisors, trainers and previous graduates, you kept going until you felt confident and competent…and you qualified.

If you have been in practice for some time, you are aware how much easier things are that used to seem so difficult.

You have moved from unconscious incompetence to conscious incompetence, to conscious competence, to unconscious competence. It is the same process we go through in learning EVERYTHING.

The sooner you start doing something differently, the sooner it will become unconscious and easy- and you'll wonder how it was ever a problem in the first place.

Growing your business, expanding your income, creating a niche, saying no to less than dream clients, getting comfortable in money conversations, charging what you're worth... are all changes we can respond to in this way.

It isn't that you can't change or that you lack the 'natural' ability to change (or you're too old to change!).

It's just that you have to get over the early stages of discomfort brought on by change...to remember this is the natural way we ALL learn as human beings.

Fear of being visible and standing out

Doing things differently takes us more deeply out of our own comfort zone when it also takes us out of the comfort zone of our peers.

There's a term known as Tall Poppy Syndrome, defined in Wikipedia as *"a social phenomenon in which people of genuine merit are resented, attacked, cut down, or criticised because their talents or achievements elevate them above or distinguish them from their peers"*.

And we fear it.

When we come up with excuses for not doing things differently, like, "I don't know anyone else who..." it comes from a place of wanting to remain within the comfort of our peer group.

Yet if we don't stand out, we don't get noticed; and if we aren't noticed people don't find us and want to work with us; and if people don't find us and want to work with us, we have to work really hard to go and find them; which means more time and marketing expense than you really need.

The way to handle this is to shatter the illusion that you 'don't know anyone else who…..' by recognising that you are not alone in wanting what you want.

Find an environment of like-minded people who also want to: build a fulfilling and successful business; charge what they are worth; create a legacy of power for their children; share their gifts more widely; live their life purpose in integrity and with authenticity; be successful.

There are tens of thousands of people the world over who want what you want.

You are in a vast field of tall poppies, reaching for the light and the air that will allow you to thrive. Put your head up and you will see them waving to you, welcoming you into the light.

MONEY AND RISK….

"I'll make enough money first, then……"

This is the queen of all procrastination excuses. So often, you hear people make promises to themselves, to their spouses, to their coaches…that when they have put by enough money, they will:

- ➢ invest in a coach or mentor
- ➢ take actions to build their business

When I hear a sentence starting that way, I know that someone is postponing their success to a time when they will have to make the same decision from a position of even less money – or they will never take those decisions.

I've done it myself –and I have seen it in clients.

There are two ways this occurs:

1.   You still have the day job (not what you want to be doing, but what you feel you have to be doing) and plan to build a cushion big enough to sustain you in the early stages of your new business...plus, do some of the groundwork for that business, while someone else is footing the bill. It all sounds great in theory.

2.   You are in full time practice and plan to save money until you have enough to invest in expanding it. It sounds sensible.

In both cases, you are in deep self-denial and that self-denial is driven by fear.

In the first case, whether you put money by for when you take the big decision to leap or you run a business alongside the day job, it can become a neatly rationalised EXCUSE for not taking BIG action that drags on and on...and all the while, you are getting no closer to fulfilling your dreams.

It is fear that holds you here and it is the same fear that holds you back from making effective business building decisions when you DO leap. You have to resolve that fear NOW.

In the second, this is just plain illogical. The reason you need to make this big change in your business is because you are short of one of two things: – time; or money.

If you know you need to make this change in order to increase your income, you have to make the investment FIRST.

Thinking more money will miraculously appear without making the investment in a coach or mentor is like opening a shop and thinking you will buy some stock after customers come in and pay for it. It won't happen.

If you know you need to make this change in order to prevent burnout…it is possible that you could save the money before investing; but it just increases the pressure you feel to work harder and longer – and pre-empt the very burnout you want to avoid.

Bite the bullet. Do it sooner, rather than later.

The only doubt in your mind is not about who you are investing in. It is whether you are willing to do what it takes and, as I've said and will continue to say, this has nothing to do with ability and everything to do with self-belief.

The thing that holds you back is the same thing you work on with clients, day in, day out. You know, because you see it, how effortlessly that can shift with the right support.

So what are you waiting for?

WORK LIFE BALANCE

Perhaps a life time on the employee treadmill; or the evidence of other entrepreneurs you know or hear about; convinces you that you have to trade a great income for a great home and social life.

This is not true. It is not a choice you have to make.

The implicit and explicit reframe between the covers of this book is all about choice – choice to work full time and earn a great income or to work part time and earn a great income.

Either way, once you set your intention, the model laid out in this book can fulfil either objective. I personally know 7 figure business women who work 4 day weeks, 3 week months and 10 month years.

This is your business and you are in control of your path to freedom, ease and creating a new model that works for you, for your family and for your bank balance.

Once you know what marketing tools work best for each stage of your business, when to outsource, what to outsource and how to decide who to outsource to; you can create the business that works for you – full time or part time; with an income far in excess of what you may currently be making in your existing work - full or part time.

Physician, heal thyself

When I started to achieve the success I wanted in my business, I was working with a fabulous high end coach and mentor and she was teaching me great stuff - in a way that no-one else had ever shown me.

However, early on, it seemed like I needed her on hand every day to deal with the self-doubt that shrouded me from the success I was capable of.

I had so many great ideas and wanted to turn my business around and fulfil my vision with purpose and passion, but my subconscious was kicking and screaming and demanding that I resist the changes I was planning.

I really wanted to work with another hypnotherapist to help me manage my fears and overcome them; but I was in uncharted territory. I knew from casual conversations with colleagues that there was a sense of 'wait and see' about what I was doing.

I didn't doubt the sincerity of others in their desire for my success, but I sensed they were waiting to be fully convinced.

So, it simply didn't seem possible for me to work with anyone to manage my fears over something they doubted themselves. It was like being afraid of flying and wanting help with my fear from someone who doubted that it was safe to fly!

I sometimes thought…if only I could be my own client.

Then it dawned on me. I could.

I had all the tools I needed and, although it is often harder to see – and change – what is holding us back, than it is to see – and help change – what is holding others back, I realised that it wouldn't hurt to employ some of the great tools I had for my own benefit.

There was no harm in trying, at any rate!

What I discovered was that, with my own skills and abilities, I was able to shift from a very high emotional state to a much calmer, motivated place, where I was able to act on what was being asked of me.

It freed me from the fear and paralysis that was preventing me from taking the actions that would take me out of overwhelm and propel me towards achievement of my goals.

Here's what I did. You might like to try it yourself.

A little self-help exercise

In order to do exactly what I did, you need to apply some "Freestyle' hypnotherapy scripting skills and you need to be able to record your own audios. I use a wonderful free tool called Audacity, but smartphones have some wonderful apps which can produce the same level of quality.

For those of you, who have no idea what "Freestyle' hypnotherapy scripting is and would like a simple set of 'how to' instructions, you can download this for free from my website at *http://shirleybillson.com/downloads-from-reframe.*

Exercise: Self Help

1. Start the recording and begin talking. Indulge your 'story' and give yourself full permission to complain, cry, describe the 'problem,' describe how you want it to be different… all without censorship.

2. After around 10 – 15 minutes you will enter a repetitive state and you can stop recording, knowing you are sufficiently emotionally spent.

3. Pause, breathe deeply, shift your energy (imagine a client about to walk through the door for a session).

4. Play the recording back, this time listening and taking notes as the therapist, ideally using the 'Freestyle' hypnotherapy scripting method.

5. Hit record again – and record your hypnosis session as the hypnotherapist.

The very fact that the 'client session' is a recording provides a dissociation that makes it easier to listen as you would to a client – (compared to challenging your negative self-talk in the moment!)

Whenever I felt low, emotional, doubtful, I would play my own hypnosis audio – and it worked brilliantly!

****

Whether you are an NLP'er, a solution focused hypnotherapist, a regression hypnotherapist, a CBT'er, or something else, constructing your own self-help regime, will increase both your sense of self-awareness and your confidence in your own expertise.

Above all, it can help you find where the really stubborn blocks are that require external support to resolve; and go some way to resolving them.

Never underestimate your own talent!

For more self-help exercises, visit

http://shirleybillson.com/downloads-from-reframe.

CHAPTER THREE:
REFRAME 2 - MONEY

CHARGING BY THE HOUR

Here's the 'recipe for success' I see most hypnotherapists working to:

1. Start at a low to medium hourly rate because that will bring new business through the door.

2. Allow business to simmer for a few years (aka evolve).

3. Start getting lots of referrals, bringing down the cost of customer acquisition (aka cost of getting a client).

4. Put prices up (maybe) or have a waiting list of clients (aka nirvana).

It's exactly the model I started out with. It's what my training school 'prepared' me for. It's what everybody else seemed to be doing. So I did it too.

However, because of its' complete dependence on number of client hours worked, it's a model that has considerable flaws. It means you risk:

➢ an absolute ceiling on potential income

➢ a risk of burnout

➢ never being able to accurately predict next month's income (never mind next year's!)

I have watched esteemed colleagues (the *successful* ones) use this model and go down the burnout route. They routinely got sick, needing to take regular days, weeks and sometimes months off – and were desperately trying to build extra income by creating other avenues for business outside their consulting rooms (not as an 'instead of' but as an 'as well as' – and creating more of an opportunity for overwhelm and burnout).

In my case, I refused to entertain burnout as an option, so I would beaver away at creating passive income with online programmes – thinking (incorrectly) that, if I learned enough about how to drive online traffic to my website(s), this would provide a passive income and I could just see a handful of clients (the ones I wanted to see), giving me the precious free time I so wanted to create in my life.

The trouble was, I spent so much time online, investing in internet marketing programmes and products, writing articles, blogs, creating videos and learning how to build web sites, that I neglected to build the other part of my business – working with clients 1:1 – and, you've guessed it, I had less free time, not more.

Instead of making more money, I made less. Much less. I went from one year making £48,000 gross (around $75,000) seeing just hypnotherapy clients – to half that seeing some clients and selling some online programmes.

And my income took on a rollercoaster pattern of unpredictable ups and downs that made it difficult to plan for anything.

I knew something had to change. I just couldn't figure out what – and no-one I knew in any hypnotherapy training school or official body was providing anything that offered a workable alternative solution.

I was almost at my wit's end.

Thankfully, I learned how to value the transformations I made possible for my clients, so that I could create programmes that people would be willing to invest in.

Once I did that, I could feel confident offering from a place of integrity and I was able to consign the hourly paid model to the bin.

IT'S NOT ABOUT THE MONEY

Many times I have heard people say this…as a way of earning a public stamp of approval for the fact that finally you are doing something rewarding that you want to do, instead of something soulless that someone else wants you to do.

If you hear yourself saying or thinking something like, "it's only money" or, "the money's not important, I just want to help people," or "money isn't spiritual," or "charging too much is exploitative," I urge you to ask yourself,

"Is that really true – or am I just afraid of playing big and failing?"

I'll come onto the value of you and pricing of services later in the book, but for now, I want to stir things up a little.

Unless you are the recipient of a huge amount of passive income – or genuinely fulfilled and happy to live in a yurt and eat berries for the rest of your life, I urge you to face up to the role money has in your life – and accept that you are worthy of having more of it; without some arbitrary limit or sanction on how much.

It may be unlikely that money is your primary motivation for practising hypnotherapy. You, like me, I suspect, have a passion for practising it and playing a part in the astonishing transformations that are possible.

However, just because you want to help people doesn't mean you have to become impoverished or limit your income potential to do so. If you've chosen it as a living and you're good at it, why should you feel ashamed of charging what you're worth and making a great living doing it?

Why should *anyone* challenge – or resent – you charging what you are worth and making a great living?

And what is the value of the arbitrary measure called 'enough' or 'reasonable' or 'too much'? For whom???

It is not a crime to want to live comfortably, go on holiday, work part time, pay for your parents care, your children's education, or to shower friends and loved ones with gifts or establish a charitable foundation of your own if you choose to.

Would you choose impoverishment or a capped income for you friends? For your family? For your clients?

I suspect not. So why might you be choosing it for yourself?

The truth is that, however successful or unsuccessful you currently believe yourself to be, you are capable of so much more and many more people will benefit from you stepping into a financially enriched, expanded place.

I have come to believe that money is the final piece of the jigsaw that connects you with the achievement of your life purpose.

When you hold an uneasy relationship with money, when you fear its' lack or cling to it tightly, you are out of alignment with yourself and the universe. You are attaching an emotional meaning to money that reflects your relationship with the world.

If you fear you will lose it, or will not be able to have it, it is not money you do not trust – it is you. When you feel it is worthless or put it on a pedestal, you are disconnected, not just from it, but from yourself too.

Money will flow to you when you trust and value yourself enough to know you are worthy. When you love yourself and value what money can bring to you - and do for you - and how it can be the enabler of the magic you are here to create in the world.

Accepting and honouring money means feeling comfortable with a fee or a salary that honours you and is an expression of the value you place upon yourself. That usually means demanding more than you currently do.

You are not a lesser person for charging or earning less…but you are not in alignment with yourself or the love the universe has for you…when you do so.

As an entrepreneur in a helping profession, you are making a stand for yourself and others and you owe it to life (for your sake and for the sake of your children) to charge what you are worth…and to honour, respect and encourage others to do the same.

Know that money is there for you, that it is possible to achieve what you want to achieve, that you don't have to wait for someone else to tell you it's ok, or give you a break, or a hand-out, or a leg up.

If you are in a difficult place and all society seems to tell you that you can't change, it can be hard to hear what I am saying and act on it with any conviction; but, in my view, loving yourself means listening to your heart's desires, giving yourself permission to express them, and the encouragement to fulfil them.

This, after all, is what you choose to do when you love someone else.

Listen to your heart and your dreams and be brave enough to follow them. Love yourself enough to listen to yourself.

Love yourself rich.

When you do, everything begins to change.

IT'S GREEDY TO CHARGE MORE

"Shouldn't I be lucky/grateful to 'earn' £70 per hour?" might be the kind of thought running in the background of your mind; or it might be the kind of thought you assume is running through your prospective client's mind – or your friends' minds, even though you know full well that you are not earning anything like £70 per hour or £50 per hour.

Once you tot up the value of all the client facing hours over the year, then deduct your expenses, you might be grateful to see more than £10,000 – which equates to less than £6 per hour if you assume an average 48 week year and a 35 hour week.

Even if you aren't seeing clients for 35 hours, add in all the time you spend working at your computer, preparing for sessions, networking, attending supervision and CPD. It all counts!

You are worth more than around £6 per hour, or even £12 per hour, or even £24 per hour.

The trouble is, on some level, you might feel greedy for wanting more, especially when other equally talented professionals are charging the same or less in the clinics where you practise.

However, instead of comparing yourself with counsellors, or nutritionists, or acupuncturists, for example, why not compare yourself with health consultants or the chief executive of an ethical organisation you admire, like a charity, for example?

Play the 'act as if' game. Act as if you are the chief executive of a multi 6 or 7 figure ethical business or charity, for example; act as if you are a millionaire hypnotherapist. Act as if you are someone who values themselves and their own brilliance.

It helps to elevate your own thinking around your value – and position you in your own mind and in the minds of your clients - as offering a higher level or service.

Act as if until it becomes reality. Remember, the brain can't distinguish between what we imagine and what is real.

It's wrong to love money

It is almost obscenely pornographic to put money and love together. Money is, perhaps, the last taboo, especially within the middle classes. The very subject brings emotional resistance, such as guilt, shame, fear, loathing, disgust.

Yet, love for money does not mean worship of money. (That is no more reasonable to assume than attaching the same 'rationality' to someone adoring trees, silk or the colour blue).

If you are already motivated to transform and make possible wonderful things for others – to help them live their lives with expanded joy and possibility - it will not change when you start to make great money doing it – and *want* to make great money doing it; and love making great money doing it.

What *will* change is that you will feel more **secure** – and when you feel secure, you can start creating a bigger, better relationship with money.

Money – and the desire for more of it - can be the catalyst for change that pushes you to be more than you are allowing yourself to be right now.

Money has the power to stretch you - to be uncomfortable, to do more, to do things differently; if you allow it.

And when you realise the creation of money is within your power, through your love for yourself, through your love for others and through your love for money itself, anything is possible.

Once you and it are equal partners in the relationship, you will be able to reach out to bigger and wider audiences in a way you can only dream of now.

More is possible. Much more.

CHARGING MORE MEANS EXPLOITING AND EXCLUDING PEOPLE WHO 'CAN'T AFFORD IT

Many of us believe, subconsciously or consciously, that we have to choose between being emotionally rewarded and being financially rewarded; and, if we make money doing what we love that involves helping people, we are somehow cheating them, abusing them – or not remaining in integrity with ourselves.

For some reason, we start to feel guilty about 'charging too much,' about 'excluding' people who can't pay and who 'need' us. There is something almost dirty about the thought that you could actually treat this as a business at all. Somehow it is perceived as ok to make a 'reasonable' living, but not to create a 'lucrative' business.

These are myths with no evidence to support them.

Long term, you can help more people by charging higher than by charging low. Pricing low means you most likely end up helping fewer people than you otherwise could.

How could this be, I hear you ask?

I'll cover pricing in a later chapter, but in simple terms...the more you charge individuals for exclusive time with you, the more freedom (and time) you have to create lower priced entry points for people who could never afford you otherwise – like books and group workshops or inexpensive self-hypnosis and self-study programmes.

All the while you charge low fees, you are compelled to fill as many hours as possible with 1:1 clients...those who cannot afford you at this price point will never afford you, and, knowing this, you may feel tempted to offer even lower discounted rates to those people....keeping you stuck and still not reaching all the people who would truly benefit from your expertise.

It is no secret that, no matter how many hours you work, you only have so many hours available to you. It simply is not possible, working with your existing model, to reach more people than the hours you have in your week.

There's a much bigger story here around the assumptions we make regarding what people can afford and what they are willing to pay; and whether we even have a right to decide that for others before they have a chance to decide for themselves.

If you've ever thought – even for a moment – that charging more for what you do means making money out of helping people – and that is exploitative, I think you are wrong.

I have come to believe – from experience and from working with others with massively altruistic goals, that you can indeed make money, be ethical and help more people than you currently do – if you are willing to treat what you do as a business; if you are willing to confront your belief systems around money; if you are willing to do things differently.

The moment when this really hit home for me was when I told a friend I had been for Reiki and explained how much I loved it and how amazing I thought it was. She responded that she was trained in Reiki, but it was clear that she felt it immoral to charge someone to receive it. She explained that it was a 'gift' from the universe and it was therefore *wrong* to charge money to share that gift. Somehow this meant the person I was receiving Reiki from was unethical.

I thought about this for a while…and then realised that my friend wasn't practising Reiki AT ALL. This gift she said she had was not being shared with anyone.

She, like you and me and most people I know, had bills that needed paying. She had a car that needed fuel and servicing, a house that needed mortgage payments, children who needed feeding and clothing…and so on.

So she chose to do something else she could get paid for…rather than share the gift she was given; and that meant that NO-ONE was being helped.

Chapter Four:
Reframe 3 - Possibility

"Our deepest fear is not that we are inadequate.
Our deepest fear is that we are powerful beyond measure.
It is our light, not our darkness
That most frightens us.

We ask ourselves
Who am I to be brilliant, gorgeous, talented, fabulous?
Actually, who are you not to be?
You are a child of God.

Your playing small
Does not serve the world.
There's nothing enlightened about shrinking
So that other people won't feel insecure around you.

We are all meant to shine,
As children do.
We were born to make manifest
The glory of God that is within us.

It's not just in some of us;
It's in everyone.

And as we let our own light shine,
We unconsciously give other people permission to do the same.

As we're liberated from our own fear,
Our presence automatically liberates others" (Williamson, 1992).

YOU ARE AN EXPERT

Whatever your level of experience as a hypnotherapist, you are an expert.

As long as you are one step ahead of the clients who come to you, you are an expert...an expert at taking them the next step they want to go.

Plus, you know way more than you think.

All those hours and years you spent doing something else, before coming to this point, have not been wasted. Every shred of experience and learning you have acquired – however you have acquired it – contribute to the unique expertise you have; that makes working with YOU so much more valuable than working with someone else.

No experience, good or bad, is wasted. Recognising your expert status can mean embracing parts of you and your life that you had thought gone, or you had thought valueless, or you had associated with something you wanted to let go of.

For a long time I resisted acknowledging – or using- any of my skills as a business woman or a marketing professional. I had set up my own company before. I had been a director of an advertising agency when I was 29. I had an MA in Marketing.

However, I had also been made redundant and been fired more than once – and felt like none of what I had achieved had any value, because it didn't achieve success on any terms I now wanted. So I decided none of this was relevant – and I associated ALL of it with a life I no longer cared for. Now I was a hypnotherapist and I didn't care for corporate life or business practice.

This was a mistake. I had created an association between my own natural skills and abilities and environments that frustrated me and starved my creativity and humanity.

My subconscious had done what it did best – created a pattern; but this pattern was holding me back from creating a new one, one that was reflective of a life lived on my terms according to my strengths and my rules.

Once I realised this, I was able to reframe my perspective. I was able to see the expert status this gave me – and realise I could express this expert status in an entirely new and creative way. I could combine this with my passion for hypnotherapy, my desire to run my own business and work the hours I wanted, working with people I loved, who valued what I had to offer.

I was an expert all along – an expert in being me, with all the skills and experience that entailed, which included not only business expertise and hypnotherapy skill, but included experience as a single mother, as a divorcee, as a mature woman starting a fresh life, as a woman crafting a future for herself and for her children, as a woman crafting a life different than the one my parents had led me to believe was possible for me, as a woman who had experienced loss, had experience disastrous relationships and successful relationships, as a woman who had kept falling down, but got back up again.

I was an expert in being me – and you are an expert in being you. It is time to embrace ALL that you are and give yourself permission to enmesh it with the skills that you bring as a hypnotherapist or healer.

Vision, Passion and Purpose

There are heroes on every street and in every town; but all the while they play safe and stay small, they limit their gifts to a handful of people in their neighbourhood – and that seems like a tragedy for the rest of the world, who never get to share in their brilliance.

Your core hypnotherapy skills create amazing transformations; but the real value is in you.

So many people talk about vision, passion and purpose, yet few are fully awakened to all three in a way that allows them to embrace them and create a pathway to success on their terms.

For me, it starts with passion; and I'm guessing, if you are reading this book, your passion is in some part aligned with your hypnotherapy. It certainly is for me.

However, connecting with your passion is just the first step. Whilst it is the foundation stone for building your successful and fulfilling business, you can't expect the rest of the proverbial house to be built by itself just because you lay that first stone.

You have to give yourself permission to dream a little. Consider the miracle question and how it relates to your own life, your own business, your own dreams and aspirations. Create a vision for yourself; and write it down.

I always say to my clients – "it doesn't matter if you don't believe it's possible or achievable, just pretend it is."

This is no time or place to think small, to limit your responses to 'enough' or 'acceptable' or even 'good.' If you can't give yourself permission to even think bigger, you will never open the door of possibility to something greater.

The scale of your success – and I mean fulfilling success on your terms, not on somebody else's terms – is limited by your willingness to give voice to your dreams as they relate to your passion.

I've done exercises around this with many clients during VIP day intensives - and the results are nearly always a surprise to both of us. They discover that what they thought they wanted to achieve was often driven by someone else's agenda (or their perception of someone else's agenda); and not actually what they wanted at all. They discover the things they really want to do relate to hidden dreams or neglected pleasures.

Once you figure out what your vision really is, you sometimes discover a deeper passion that is even truer to your purpose than what you originally brought to the table.

It can be disconcerting for a while, because it challenges the very core of what you thought you were doing. It can throw your structure, your order, your model of how things should be into disarray. It's temporary though.

As you allow it room to breathe, it takes on greater form – and that's when it starts to reveal the link with life purpose.

However, this is an evolving process that you need to allow to happen, all the while remaining open to the learning your vision and your passion show you.

As your vision begins to take on more shape and structure, it comes full circle to something much, much bigger than you ever imagined at the outset. This is where the magic happens.

The reason it is so important to me – and to my clients – is that it allows you to feel fully authentic, to act only out of integrity and to remain totally connected to what matters to you and who you are.

Be prepared. Big changes happen when you do this.

In my experience with clients, it has a habit of creating such major shifts in people's lives that they change direction completely, they move house and home, they let go of work and relationships that no longer serve them, they build businesses of their own, they resurrect interests that are vital to their sustained energy and passion.

They truly become themselves.

You will already have ascertained that I am not only interested in helping people make more money. There are many books that will tell you that.

What matters deeply to me is that your financial success is aligned fully with your unique gifts and your individual brilliance.

When you figure out just what it is that makes you unique, what your true passion and purpose is – you can get clear on your personal vision of success and make it happen.

Plus, when you show up more as yourself, you free up oceans of energy to focus on what really matters and create the spiritual and financial wealth you are seeking.

That makes it possible to create a realisable vision for success – with timelines and associated goals that bring dreams and desires to life and make them achievable.

****

Look around you in any town. How many hairdressers do you see? Cafes? Bars?

Lots. And does each of them offer principally the 'same service'? Yes. But do each of us prefer one café, hairdresser or bar over another? Yes.

Why? Because something about the entire experience, the ambience, our taste, our style, the people we hang out with and the other people who use the service….all contribute to a 'unique' experience that we might not be able to accurately describe, but means we 'just like it' better.

Hypnotherapists are no different….so, even if there are 6 or 60 other hypnotherapists in your town, each of you has a unique style and personality that is conveyed through your work and your interaction with clients.

Which means that some will love you and can't stand someone else – and vice versa.

What prospective clients are looking for is someone who they like the look of and someone they like the 'sound of.'

They are picking you in the same way we pick friends and partners – based on initial impressions and gut instincts – about whether this person is my kind of person. They are looking for rapport before they meet you.

Everything you say, every colour you choose, every photo you use, tells people about who you are…and you want it to be authentically you; but you also need to be clear about your dream client and your niche; otherwise your marketing copy and design tries to do too much, tries to appeal to everyone – and can't.

So you end up with fewer clients than you might otherwise have; and you may make the common assumption that the reason for this is that a) your prices are too high b) you need more qualifications and experience!

Your challenge is to fully embrace your uniqueness – and let it shine.

Lifting the veil on the blind-spot

In my years working as both a hypnotherapist and a mentor, I have become more and more aware of the blind spot that many of us have around our ability to know who we are and what we are capable of.

I have also seen the veil lifted with such exquisite ease and delicious results that I urge you to consider whether you, too, might have this blind spot.

The blind spot exists around acknowledging and expressing our true needs and desires with unashamed honesty and lack of apology.

"This is who I am and this is what I need" seems to be the final hurdle to the success we crave and the acceptance we want; and this hurdle exists both in people who know they lack confidence and those who think they have confidence.

The clue to whether the blind spot exists is in the frustration we feel in not achieving what we want to achieve. For some, it might be not making enough money or attracting enough clients; for others, it might be not feeling able to trust others to do things to our standards; or trying to do it all.

One pushes us in to overwhelm, the other pushes us to despair.

Both are evidence of the blind spot; and, whichever camp you fall into, you will be able to present reams of evidence for the truth of your experience.

You will either have endless examples of asking others for support or assistance and being let down, so you give up asking and find it easier to do it yourself; or you will have repeated stories of trying and failing to achieve the success that seems to come so easily to others, only to be disappointed, so you just become convinced that you don't have what it takes.

In both cases, the overwhelming evidence that this is the truth will result in you taking the default action that assumes it is true – and result in it being confirmed. It will hold you back from the change you desire – for greater ease and an ability to spend more time celebrating your accomplishments than pushing yourself on and on in pursuit of something that never arrives.

Express your Needs and Desires

Resolution of the blind spot requires clarity on two things:

1. what it is you really want

2. boundaries

Lack of clarity on the first guarantees there will be issues with the second. If, after all, you don't know exactly what it is you want, how can you be crystal clear on instructions, requests, goals and projected outcomes?

And if you're not clear, this leads to vague instructions, vague requests, vague goals and vague projected outcomes; which lead to frustrated and frustrating relationships, disappointment and inconsistent success.

If you are confused about what it is you really want, you are guaranteed not to get it.

Lack of clarity on the second guarantees there will be problems achieving the first. If you do know what you want, but aren't crystal clear about expressing that to others, for whatever reason - perhaps because you assume they should know, or you don't like to ask, or think you shouldn't have to ask, or you think 'everybody should know that' – then you will be thwarted in the degree of success you achieve.

It is surprising how many of us, especially women, really aren't clear on what we want – or in expressing what we want. We can get so good at fitting in, not rocking the boat, not wanting to upset anyone, valuing compromise above self-fulfilment, that it can seem like an impossible task – and almost unnatural - to start saying what we really want.

WHERE TO BEGIN

In my experience, the easiest way to begin is by looking at areas of frustration at work or at home. Who – or what – is a recurrent source of annoyance, frustration or resignation?

Instead of making assumptions about what another person/organisation will do or say, based on previous experience, consider two things:

1. What would you actually like to say to them, or what you would like to ask for, that you aren't asking for or saying now?

2. How would you really like to respond to something they generally say or do – in a way that you aren't responding now?

In neither case am I suggesting a rant or an out of control venting of frustration, in which you 'let them have it.'

Instead, imagine a calm, grown up conversation and/or response is possible, adult to adult (irrespective of how you or they might have behaved in the past).

Consider exactly what you would like to do or say, so you can calmly express your needs and desires in any particular situation. Now act on it.

Many times I have had this conversation with clients who have doubted, challenged and resisted what I am suggesting; but, because they want a different outcome, they also come round to the acceptance that they have to do something different; that they can no longer allow themselves to take responsibility for what someone else does or says. So they may as well stop and try to please themselves instead.

They can only be accountable to themselves – and trying to please everybody might be desirable sometimes but is NEVER achievable. EVER.

Christine, for example, reported how her children stopped being so demanding - and started valuing boundaries. Clients stopped cancelling and turning up late. Her husband started telling her he loved her (often) after 10 years of marriage when he had barely uttered it more than a handful of times before. He started getting dinner ready before she came home (unheard of).

Jane, who worked with her husband, found he stopped sulking and complaining so much – and started appreciating and supporting. They went from the brink of separation to dating again (after 25 years of marriage). She stopped trying to do everything and stopped feeling responsible every time someone else made a mistake. Instead of trying to fix everything for everybody, she asked them how they were going to fix things for themselves.

They NEVER regretted stepping into a place of empowerment and beginning to express what it was they wanted for them.

To their credit, however much they doubted the outcome before they took action, when they did act on it, they were always astounded by what ensued; and so was I.

<u>If you want people to feel empowered, you need to empower yourself</u>

If you care deeply about your clients fulfilling their biggest potential, living their life purpose and stepping into the possibility presented by their unique strengths, you have to give yourself permission to empower yourself fully first.

"I will not let anyone walk through my mind with their dirty feet." Mahatma Ghandi

I can remember hanging onto the fragments of a failed marriage for way too long...thinking it was best for my son, thinking I would not cope on my own; yet the moment I faced up to what I really wanted and took the decision to leave , my son was able to relax into being himself (instead of being stuck in the middle of a daily warzone); my ex was able to find the partner who really suited him; I was able to find the partner who was perfect for me, to live where I really wanted, to learn what I wanted to learn, to build the business I wanted to build.

The resentment and bitterness I had held within my marriage dissolved and I managed to maintain far more amicable relations with my ex than friends who had NOT made the same kind of active choice regarding what they wanted.

In my business, once I stopped fearing what clients would think if I let them know where they were holding themselves back, I started attracting more of the dream clients I loved. When they were challenged, though they may have resisted at first, they subsequently thanked me for pulling them forward.

Stepping into the business I want for myself makes it possible for me to enable others to step into the business they want for themselves.

I am eternally grateful and blessed. It may have come late in life…but it is all the sweeter for that.

If you are still confused about what you really want, download the free exercise, Unleash Your Core Brilliance via http://shirleybillson.com/downloads-from-reframe/.

Chapter Five:
Reframe 4 – Being Good Enough

Perhaps some of you might be thinking something along the lines of…"well, that's alright for you, but I don't have that kind/level of knowledge/ experience/ background/ skill/ money/ expertise."

It doesn't really matter which of the interchangeable words is most relevant for you; and, however you might dress them up in 'fact' (remember, the brain doesn't know how to distinguish between fact and fiction), the truth is that these are all screaming, "I am not good enough" or "I do not know enough."

Perhaps you compare yourself with others – colleagues in your class, graduates you meet at supervision, hypnotherapists you have heard speak, hypnotherapists whose books you have read, who have appeared on TV or in your local paper or hypnotherapists whose classes you have attended.

You might even spread your net of comparisons to include other therapists, counsellors, health and wellness practitioners, coaches, entrepreneurs – and you might use all of this comparison to say or think, something along the lines of:

"I'm not ready yet"

"I don't know enough"

"I'm not that clever"

"I'm not that confident"

"I need more experience"

"I don't have money to invest"

"I need another qualification first"

"I'm not an expert"

Read that list again. Does it remind you of anything?

Your clients, perhaps?

The trouble with comparison is that, instead of using it as a great opportunity to learn, we often set up an internal competition that we will never win.

It is like trying to win a 'handsomest' or 'prettiest' competition. This kind of subjective comparison can damage your self-esteem and, whilst you can often still be a good practitioner, it truly diminishes your ability to be a great practitioner – and it has nothing to do with how clever or qualified you are.

There will always be someone who has studied more, earned more, got a better qualification, seen more clients, written more, got a better web site, etc. Good for them; but have you ever seen someone with lots of qualifications never earn a bean – or someone with only a few qualifications make millions?

Have you ever witnessed someone who you know, deep down, isn't better qualified or smarter than you…rise to the top with almost effortless ease?

It's because, instead of worrying about what they haven't got (again…remember the way the brain works on expanding our perception of what we focus on), they focus on what they want to achieve – and they find ways to make it happen.

They don't give up and they start to seek out people and places who will support them in their ambition. They work on being masters of their own mind. (Physician, heal thyself!).

You have everything you could possibly need to make a huge change in your life...you understand the mechanics of how to overcome fear; of how to challenge limiting beliefs; of how to tap into what you know - in order to discover that you have all the resources you need to live the life you want and choose different actions today than those you chose yesterday.

You do know enough and you are good enough.

Brag with style

Bragging is the new skill you need to acquire.

For many – especially those of any kind of British extraction – 'bragging' is impolite, doesn't show class, isn't necessary and is something that, if done at all, someone else needs to do on your behalf – but you NEVER do yourself.

It's time to unlearn ALL of that.

To get yourself in the swing of bragging with style, start with self-congratulation.

Whenever you achieve something, however small, be thankful for it, tell someone you know will support you and share your pride – and, if you are a social media user, post it on FB, Twitter, LinkedIn.

Better still, post it on all of them.

You know better than anyone when small things are huge achievements – and, in becoming a success being you, it's all about the personal. So, if you or one of your clients just got a breakthrough, let people know.

You don't need to break any confidentiality or name names...but you can say how excited you are that a client just drove on a motorway for the first time, or got a new job because their interview went so well – and include why this is a big deal for them!

If you get a new qualification, don't share only with your nearest and dearest. Let people know what you achieved and what it means for you, especially if the meaning is something your prospective clients can relate to.   Make it public. This is precisely where social media comes into its own.

Maybe it signifies that persistence pays off, that commitment to an outcome results in achievement of an outcome...or, perhaps, that you are now even more of an expert in a specific field of expertise.

Whatever it is, your challenge from now on (should you accept the mission!) is to get accomplished at celebrating.

➢ Getting better at celebrating your achievements internally increases your self-esteem.

➢ Getting better at celebrating your achievements externally embeds the increase in your self-esteem – and increases the confidence of others in you – and your expertise.

➢ If you are to achieve greater success, it starts with being seen to achieve greater success.

Usually, your clients are people who don't know you until they walk through a door and meet you....and that is the first opportunity you get to build rapport and start helping them achieve amazing transformations.

However, when you get better at bragging about your success, people who have been on the periphery of your world - who are connected to someone, who is connected to someone, who is connected to someone you are connected to – begin to get the opportunity to get to know you BEFORE you know them. They start creating rapport with you when you don't even know it.

And these are the 'strangers' who become your clients and your advocates.

Better still, when you celebrate things that are really important to you and who you are and what you are trying to achieve in life….these 'strangers' who are drawn into your world are your dream clients. They are drawn in by YOU and who you are in all your brilliant uniqueness.

And the more you draw new people in, the more you have to celebrate, and the more you celebrate the more new people you draw in.

Win, win, win, win, win.

This is a way to advertise without looking like you're advertising; and so much cheaper.

It's personal PR (public relations) power; and it doesn't mean you have to spend all day on social media…just one item per day that is relevant to your audience. Something like…'drank a toast to one of my wonderful clients…she just achieved her goal of getting the promotion she wanted.'

For many of us, the clients we get the best results with – and who we most love to help, are people like us, who have the same struggles and concerns.

The brain enjoys creating links and sharing your journey – small successes and large – pre-frames for potential clients what is possible for them if they consider working with you.

That's all it takes…for just 15 minutes a day.

GET POWERFUL TESTIMONIALS

I know you know testimonials work, but...

➢ Do you know how to make them powerful?

➢ Do you know when to ask for them?

➢ Do you know how to get clients to say exactly what future clients need to hear...yet all in their own words?

➢ Do you truly take in all that your client tells you?

Everyone knows the power of testimonials for persuading people to buy. They create that all important trust and rapport with people we have never met and services we have never bought.

As a consumer, as an ex advertising and marketing professional, as an MA in Marketing and as a hypnotherapist - I knew that, just as you do.

However, when it came to actually getting them when I was in clinical practice...that was another story.

In response to those I asked for, I received plenty of the type of testimonials you probably have, like:

'Shirley is very professional; hypnotherapy is great; I would unhesitatingly recommend....blah, blah' and, unprompted, I received a few of the 'you changed my life' types of testimonial - which were infinitely better for making me feel great; and for helping others see what was possible.

However, they were often really personal and, because they seemed intimate, I didn't always feel able to go back to my clients and say, "hey, do you mind if I put this on my website" because I feared that I was breaching confidentiality and betraying trust.

Plus, even when I could use them, they just didn't read as compellingly as the feedback I got in person. Lots of people would say lovely things, some would text me lovely things or send me lovely cards and gifts, and others would even say lovely things to camera... yet very few of the messages were worded in a way that added a great deal of meaning to someone reading them cold.

It was a dilemma I didn't have the answer to until I started mentoring with a high level coach...who showed me (in the way she asked ME for a testimonial) just how to get the most fabulous and authentic feedback; that demonstrates how truly amazing you can be when your clients commit to take action and make the absolute best of what you are offering them.

Getting it right has several key components – all of which make it flow beautifully.

First of all, work only with your dream clients. You know the ones. They do all that you ask of them, they turn up on time, every time. They love you...and you love them. They make your day brighter – and you go home excitedly telling your nearest and dearest (without breaching confidentiality, of course) about the amazing results they are getting, all because they are working with you.

See how easy it is to brag when you try! If only that were possible you say. You know what I'm going to say, don't you?

It is possible.

When you attract dream clients, surprise, surprise, they get the results you know are possible. And they get really excited about it...and the minute they share with you how excited they are (either via email, in person, card or text), you politely ask them if they would be willing to give you a testimonial. To which they ALWAYS say yes.

You might be thinking, "yes I've done that...but they forget or don't know what to say and I don't like to push it" – or something similar; and I've heard many people recommend you write the testimonial for your client and send it to them for approval.

Although most clients are more than happy that you do this, for me it doesn't read with the same passion. Plus, given you might still be working on the 'bragging' exercise, you may severely underplay what your client actually thinks and feels.

Offer to send them an email with a few simple and very specific questions to answer. These questions are VERY easy to answer – and they will enjoy doing it. What questions, you ask? Well, these questions – or something very similar, my friend:

1. What was the biggest challenge for you in your business before ....joining the XYZ Programme/your workshop/VIP day/etc.?

2. What have you learned to help eliminate that challenge?

3. What have you implemented so far?

4. What have been the results so far?

5. What or who are you feeling a lot of gratitude for right now?

If you are tempted to tone it down or leave out any of the questions, DON'T! That's just more evidence of the 'not good enough' and bragging avoidance syndrome that this chapter is all about.

Leave all of the questions in – and see how amazing and authentic the testimonials are; as long as you ONLY ask for them when your client has already started telling you about something amazing that they have achieved.

The questions I'm suggesting prompt your clients to really focus on what they have achieved, and what has been different for them, since they worked with you – which is, actually, really good for them too.

It extends the therapy by helping them embed their learning and even move it along a notch – as they are encouraged to look at their own achievements and their own development.

Which is all wonderful.

What it also does is reveal to you something you really need to get clear on – situational specific problems and life altering outcomes, which is where the true value of working with you shows up.

This is very important. Note that down now. It is a theme we will come back to.

For now, here's an example of just such a testimonial, which I received following the exact same formula I am proposing. I asked for it, in response to an unprompted and excited text from my client:

Case study testimonial:

Before starting Shirley's Platinum Program, my biggest challenge as a Hypnotherapist was lack of self-belief and self-worth. In a previous life I worked in a very low paid career and despite the career change and working hard to gain my new qualifications I still viewed myself as a low paid worker and felt very uncomfortable charging a large fee for my newly acquired expertise. I found myself bending over backwards for my clients, allowing them to dictate my working hours and giving large discounts and free sessions in some instances, which did nothing for my confidence in my career, I was starting to slide into overwhelm, the job was no longer enjoyable, I dreaded going in each day feeling secretly relieved when clients cancelled, this seems difficult to believe now-I was on a one way road to disaster. Since working with Shirley, I have learnt to value myself and my skills and to shake off that' low paid worker' self-imposed image. I dictate the hours I work and feel happier than ever and this can only benefit my clients, my confidence has increased in such a short time, I am enjoying the job much more, feel less pressurised to 'perform' and have had some great feedback from clients. Shirley encourages you to dream big and I am finally realising a dream that began in childhood, but not only does she encourage the dream she also gives you practical ways to plan for that success. I am so glad that I contacted Shirley and began the programme with her. I know that I am already benefiting from the investment, not just financially but in all areas of my life." Sarah Whittaker, Hypnotherapist.

TAKE CREDIT WHERE IT'S DUE

Therapists, in general, have a tendency to become fixed on the problem that their client said they came with – I'm terrified of flying, I want to lose weight, I'm having panic attacks, I have IBS, etc...

That's what we tell them we help with. However, the thing that drives them to seek help is NOT the problem.

Let me say that again, the thing that drives them to seek help is NOT the problem. It is the things that the problem prevents them doing. It is the impact on their personal lives, their careers, their work, their income, their future.

So, for example, a person who is afraid of flying actually doesn't care about it; unless it impacts them in a bigger way; like getting on a flight to Australia to see a grandchild they have never seen, like getting a promotion to a higher paid job that involves travel, like taking their business international, like rescuing a relationship by saying yes to holidays abroad.

If you re-read the testimonial above, notice all the detail Sarah provides about what was going on in her life before she worked with me; and what changed as a result of working with me. It's rich and varied, multi-dimensional – and transformational.

The benefits your clients get are just as magical.

It's vital that you can begin to accept and own more of the credit for the wider changes that take place in a client's life – and the monumental shifts that are possible for them in terms of relationships, in terms of health, in terms of career and work, in terms of finances and in terms of future potential.

When you start taking credit for more of these 'bigger' benefits, you can begin to recognise just what you are worth and describe the true value of the transformations you create – in a way that will help others who need help to find you; so they, too, can benefit from similar transformations.

That way, more people get to benefit in bigger and better ways. What could be better than that?

****

Where I used to go wrong is that I took absolutely no credit for the changes in my clients' lives beyond the solving of the problem they said they came to me for.

Any secondary benefits were lovely and I outwardly celebrated them with my client – attributing all of those shifts to them, which is right and proper.

After all, as good therapists, we are merely the facilitators and the enablers for our clients. Without their commitment, nothing changes for them; and our role is to empower them to know that THEY are the instigators of the change that occurs for them - so they can continue to grow and make even more positive changes, where they feel in control.

And that is very satisfying for all concerned.

However, the point I was really missing – that was damaging my future income and my future client's potential success – was NOT openly acknowledging and 'bragging' about all the secondary benefits that were possible for my clients, simply because they took one decision: the decision to work with me.

Once I acknowledged my part in this, it meant I was able to help future prospective clients see the possibilities too – which was as good for them as it was for me; because when prospective clients were able to see the exciting opportunities that could open up for them, simply as a result of working with me to solve their particular problem, they were able to feel more engaged, more excited, more motivated. It became a part of the reframe I was about to help them with.

We started working on outcomes and solutions before a single item of currency changed hands. I realised that it does not benefit clients to underplay possibilities. Constant positive reframing is vital to maximise what is possible for any of us.

Please do not confuse this with making false promises. I am not promising anything.

If anything, I make it more clear now, that a client is the one responsible for all the change, than I ever did in the days when I struggled to get enough clients to make ends meet.

The difference is that I now take some credit for opening up a door to possibility that has always been open, but previously never had a sign above the door. This increases my confidence in my work; and a confident practitioner is a more effective practitioner… so my clients benefit again.

An ounce of pre-framing is worth a pound of reframing

When you qualify, you are justifiably proud of our new found skill. You are excited about the possibilities that it opens up for you – a new career, a new lifestyle, an increased income, greater job satisfaction. It is thrilling stuff.

And, especially if you are a hypnotherapist, it does provoke interest in casual conversations – so it's a fun thing to tell people; and your enthusiasm probably bubbles over into every conversation. I can remember how easily I would start talking about the brain, the way it works…and how difficult it was for me to shut up about it!

However, if this is your first foray into working for yourself, you need to realise that EVERY interaction with any person, online or offline, holds the potential for new business.

When you go to networking events, or hand out your business card, or create your website…you need to get good at sharing what makes you special (you are good enough and you do know enough).

What I see, for the most part, are truly capable people hiding behind a job title so that they don't really have to talk about themselves – and God forbid, sell.

(Selling, by the way, is code for enthusiastically telling others what amazing things are possible for those who work with you – as we explored in the previous pages).

Telling people you are a hypnotherapist, however interesting a conversation that becomes, turns you into a commodity. The minute you utter the words, "I'm a hypnotherapist," you have aligned yourself – with a group of identical commodities – the hypnotherapist group.

And once someone has decided what you are, the pattern is filed in the subconscious and it makes it very, very hard, to subsequently distinguish yourself as anything else.

<u>Why does it matter?</u>

Well, let's start with the person who has never met a hypnotherapist before and doesn't think they have any reason to need one, because, they have no idea what one really does.

The moment you tell them what you do, you may get drawn into a conversation related to TV comedy, TV drama, clucking like chickens or stopping smoking – so you spend a few minutes trying to straighten out a few myths – and the most you might manage to convey is that you are a professional who helps people solve all kinds of problems, like smoking, anxiety, weight loss, etc.

They find this all very interesting – and it might, on occasion, lead to a client.

However, it might also lead to them being sufficiently interested that they Google hypnotherapy or hypnotherapists….and then they find all the other people out there, saying all the things you do…and you, perhaps, stop being YOU.

Instead, you have been silo'ed into the category of hypnotherapists, a bucket full of people with similar qualifications, treating similar problems for similar fees…so Mr or Mrs Prospective client looks for the one closest to them.

You have just disappeared into the anonymity of every other hypnotherapist with a business card and a web site.

Whereas you, of course, are unique. You have unique characteristics, unique skills and unique experience. The thing is, you may have convinced yourself that none of this matters, that none of this is relevant to your new role as a hypnotherapist – so you discount it.

Maybe it's because you don't want to have anything to do with the job you left behind, maybe you don't have an official qualification in something that you actually know a huge amount about - or maybe you just don't think it's relevant.

I'm here to tell you that it is relevant – and it is important. Devaluing your previous expertise, knowledge or experience is just another way of saying 'I'm not good enough' and 'I don't know enough.'

Here's what happened to me:

I used to go to formal networking events only, convinced that informal networking was not much more than a game of business card swapping, with little benefit in terms of new clients.

As far as the more established (and expensive!) groups, who promised all kinds of referral benefits, I covered my membership costs by treating members of the networking group itself, who each came for between one and three sessions maximum. This wasn't amazing…but I kept thinking that this would build towards my 'evolve and grow' client referral strategy.

It was only when the owner of the networking franchise said that members should expect to make at least 5 x their membership fee in the first year that I stopped to question whether this was good value. I was only just covering mine, plus a little extra – and decided it was because there were 'the wrong sort of people' in the group.

I put their failure to provide more referrals down to them not really understanding the benefits of what hypnotherapy could deliver. I decided they were resistant to complementary therapy and that the task of educating them was bigger than me.

Even as I write that, I find it incredible that I couldn't see that it was down to me to help people understand, not what hypnotherapy was capable of, but what I was capable of.

And that meant taking ownership of my own expertise, my own unique capabilities and my own brilliance.

I had to believe in myself first.

I realised that the experience I had before qualifying as a hypnotherapist – as a director of 3 companies, with an MA in marketing, with all kinds of experience – like doing TV and radio interviews, giving presentations, writing copy, providing career mentoring and training, creating web sites, advertising, brand development - not to mention life experiences like divorce, parenthood, domestic abuse, online dating. I could go on…

Instead of discounting each of these skills as irrelevant, I could choose to weave some of them into my new business, to demonstrate what I had to offer that was different – in a way that would appeal to the kinds of clients I most wanted to work with.

Once I did that (and it took more than 6 years to even consider that I could do that), I was able to start making major shifts in my business and really generating an income I felt in control of, rather than wishing and praying that enough hypnotherapy clients would pitch up.

Your own skills, whoever you are and whatever your background, are equally up to the task of creating phenomenal businesses.

Your biggest challenge is to look inside – and see what extraordinary resources you have, then to start honing them, crafting them and learning how to share with the world how this unique combination is just what your dream clients need.

Create a Vision for Success – with Timelines and Goals that Excite You.

Here's a confession. When I qualified as a hypnotherapist, I thought I was done with goal setting for good.

In fact, I was so reluctant to allow my previous ambitious business life to muddy the waters of my fresh new love for hypnotherapy that the very mention of it would bring up the drawbridge of resistance.

However, I eventually realised that, if I was to fully embrace the brilliance of me and my unique gifts, I had to get my message into the wider world. That meant I had to have a vision of where I wanted to go with it; and that meant creating goals and milestones.

It's a very simple lesson, but I was so reluctant to see it.

I used to argue that there was nothing wrong with 'just cruising, that I just wanted to do what I loved and see where it took me. I didn't want to be ambitious or set goals.

I just wanted to help people. I might end up somewhere, and I believed I didn't mind where. It seemed romantic and free.

It turned out to be neither romantic nor free. My musing was based on an assumption that the end destination would be one I wanted; but of course, if you don't choose, the end destination could be anywhere – and nowhere.

It's like going to a restaurant and telling the waiter you don't mind what you have; then when he brings you something you don't like, you wish you'd chosen; or telling a taxi driver you don't mind where he takes you until you end up in the middle of a derelict building site –and you wish you'd been specific.

I had no vision of where I wanted to go with my gifts, no destination in mind and, therefore, no direction. I was lost and going nowhere.

I learned the hard way that this was no way to share my unique brilliance and my gifts as widely as possible.

If you have the gift of writing and no-one gets to read it, it's a wasted gift. If you have a gift for singing but no-one gets to hear it, it's a wasted gift. If you have a gift for hypnotherapy and not enough people get to benefit, it's a wasted gift.

I decided, at last, to create a vision of what I wanted, based on the premise of 'if anything were possible.'

Just as you can only imagine what Bali is like before you go there, you can still choose to go based on that imagination – and take a series of steps that will get you there, until the reality of arriving shows you how it really is.

The difference between these new goals and milestones and the way I used to imagine – and resist – them; was that these were now set by me, not imposed by anyone else. They were not about fulfilling someone else's expectations or someone else's dream.

And that was an exciting, but scary, place to step into.

We so often ache for freedom only to discover we have got so accustomed to following other people's rules and allowing decisions to be made for us (by employers, family, friends, teachers, clients) that freedom is a difficult choice.

By giving yourself permission to create a thrilling vision of how you would like your business and your life to look, you take a leap of self-determination that fully enables you to be a success being you.

The key is to set your mental GPS.

EXERCISE: How to quickly create a High End State of Mind (Summerhawk)

How much is the most you've ever charged for your services?

£/$_____

Now put a zero on the end of it.

As someone who charges that amount, what do you focus on during the day?

_____
_____
_____

What do you wear?

_____
_____
_____

What do you delegate?

_____
_____

What do you get rid of in your environment?

_____
_____
_____

What do you no longer put up with/tolerate?

_____
_____
_____

Who are your colleagues?

_____

_____

_____

Who is your mentor?

_____

_____

Chapter Six:
Reframe 5 – Expert Status

Here's the good news. Being an expert doesn't mean you need to know everything there is to know. Being an expert is simply about knowing more than a lot of other people. It is not about knowing more than every other person.

Here's the really great news. When you combine expert status with your unique core brilliance, you create a competitive field of one; and that means you can confidently 'own' exactly the same topic as someone else, but it will by your fresh take on it that counts.

Never underestimate the power of you. There are many different groups who will benefit from your unique expertise, all of whom will pay handsomely. Once you're clear on the options, it's just a case of picking one you love.

Do not be put off by seeing there are other people out there who know more about a subject than you do. That comes from a place of comparison, where you always feeling the need to know more, get another qualification, notch up another year of experience.

What counts as expert knowledge?

➢ An interest in something you have read a lot about or studied just for fun.

➢ A hobby you have a passion for.

- Something you studied for, even if you didn't complete a qualification.

- Treating even one client successfully, especially if over an extended period where there was a lot of learning involved.

- Previous work based experience

- An industry or business you used to work in

- A skill you used to have.

- Life experience - e.g., parenthood, divorce, eating problems overcome, sickness or disability overcome.

- Everything counts.

How to convert expert knowledge to expert status with ease

The first thing you can do is start telling people about your expert knowledge. Start writing articles and blogs on it, consider producing some YouTube videos, maybe even buy a domain with a specialist title.

I became known as an expert in working with eating disorders, which led to me writing articles on it, getting invited to take part in a TV documentary about it and creating a whole online self-help programme around binge eating, called Ditch the Binge. I also owned domains called ProblemsWithEating.com and EatingBattles.com.

It all started with a couple of young clients who I worked with, not long after I got my hypnotherapy qualification. As with most clients when you first qualify, they just arrived randomly; and I worked with them according to my training.

I got some early successes – and they all said that I was the first person who really understood them. These vulnerable women – and, in many cases, their parents - trusted me and wanted to work with me. This led me to develop an area of expertise. I learned a lot from my clients.

I updated my professional profiles, stating that this was my area of specialism and I supplemented that claim with studying conventional methods of treating the condition (which simply meant I read more books and watched more online videos). In other words, I started to study it in a way that others probably weren't.

In a matter of a few short months, I was being described as an expert.

This meant I was asked to write articles; I was contacted by other hypnotherapists seeking guidance; I had client referrals from therapists less confident in dealing with the same problems; and I was invited to take part in a TV documentary.

I wrote an e-book, produced YouTube videos and created my own unique online programme for binge eating.

My expert status came about simply because I started telling people this is what I did.

It is not what I choose to specialise in now, though I do provide Ditch the Binge training for hypnotherapists who want additional expertise.

What I hope you see from my story is that you can CHOOSE your area of expertise and follow it up with additional study; or you can simply tell people what you already know and what experience you have that makes you an expert.

For example, you could be an expert in corporate stress, an expert in coming through the other side of redundancy, an expert in losing weight, overcoming insomnia or alcoholism, an expert in pain-free childbirth, an expert in bereavement....you get the picture.

The point is that you know so much more than you think you do; and you don't need to collect qualifications to prove your worth.

****

Some of us just love to study...and there is nothing wrong with expanding your knowledge, your skills and your expertise.

When you qualify, you are expected to commit to continuing professional development, to refresh your skills, to be in supervision, to engage in a process of lifelong learning.

Quite right too.

However, what I sometimes see is hypnotherapists collecting more and more qualifications and letters after their name, in a way to either bolster their confidence...because they don't believe they know enough to treat certain types of condition, certain types of client...or in the mistaken belief that these new qualifications will result in more clients.

I do recognise that extra study and qualifications can, indeed, result in increased confidence and, sometimes, in new clients.

However, many hypnotherapists with a lot of qualifications, certificates, diplomas and letters after their name are struggling to capitalise effectively on their learning, despite their passion for what they do – and their brilliance at it.

Meanwhile, people who are willing to share their own stories and their own experience, without necessarily proclaiming expert status, have started, knowingly or unknowingly, to act 'as if' they are expert...simply by sharing.

That willingness to step into a bigger arena by sharing learning along the way - contributes to articles, blogs, books, press, publicity and public speaking and more. Intended or not, it soon starts to be translated as expertise, or expert status.

There comes a point when you have to believe you are ready to run with what you know. Just sharing the journey can be enough.

However, achieving expert status is not enough to achieve greater financial success.

The next step is to know how to make that work for you in your business.

Chapter Seven:
Reframe 6 - Niche Matters

To benefit from your expert status, you need a niche; but not just any niche. You need a lucrative one.

Niche is such a bandied about word, you'd think it would be a simple thing to get right. Nothing could be further from the truth.

However, let's be clear about why it matters to get it right. In fact, let's be clear about why it matters more than anything else – and why, if you get this right, everything else gets easier.

"If you get your niche right, half of your work is done. When your niche is right, everything is easier after that. Much easier. Marketing works better. Customers come out of the woodwork". (Pagan)

People often confuse expert status or expertise with niche. However, they are not one and the same.

A true test of whether you are working within a true niche or not is that, when asked, you can say precisely what kind of people you specialise in working with – and in what set of circumstances; in a way that allows your dream clients to identify themselves – without lengthy additional clarification or explanation.

For example, my own niche is expressed in a single sentence (also known as the elevator pitch). "I help both entrepreneurial hypnotherapists and healers to create rewarding businesses for themselves; and professionals, who are trapped in well-paying jobs they hate, to find the courage and the means to escape".

Contrast this with what I used to think was a niche: "I help people with eating disorders"

The first example is narrow and specific. It gives some clue to the aspirations and the desires of my niche in a way that relates to an individual, not a group; and it provides clarity about the kind of outcomes those ideal clients will be seeking. The second is vague – it defines the problem but not the person or the outcome desired (assuming this is implicit).

This is where most people go wrong – myself included. When I said I helped people with eating disorders, I was telling people something about my expert status, but NOTHING about the kind of people who would be ideally suited to work with me; or what they might want to achieve as a result of working with me.

Describing a niche effectively helps your prospective niche client to identify with you, to feel like you really know them, that you truly are an expert in their unique problem; because when we have a problem, we never think of ourselves as one of a large faceless group.

We usually feel alone, like no-one else understands and no-one else suffers. Defining and describing a niche well says, "I understand YOU personally and the specific problem you are having which is different to everyone else with this problem"

I knew I could help anyone with eating disorders and I didn't want to narrow my niche because I thought it would alienate potential clients, meaning I would have fewer of them. So, I thought I was appealing equally to men, to women, to young, to old, to career people, to creatives, to stay at homes.

By contrast, as long as you follow some simple rules, which I will reveal shortly, you will discover that the narrower the niche, the greater the opportunities for expert status, for increased income and for a successful business.

In my case, I would have been far better off identifying my niche as high achieving career women with eating issues. (See how much easier it is to imagine a real person with that description?).

Overcome resistance

One of the key reasons I hear people shying away from choosing a lucrative niche is that they will not be able to serve all the people who 'need' them.

I used to think I was working with niche, but I wasn't quite getting it right (and that meant I wasn't fully committing to it), so I gave it up.

I used to say I specialised in working with people who had eating disorders. I kept it broad (even though it felt narrow to me). I didn't dare say women in case that alienated men. I didn't dare say women over 40 in case I missed out on all the young women who 'needed' me.

I didn't dare say I ONLY worked with people who had eating disorders in case I alienated ALL the people I could help (OCD, anxiety, panic attacks, depression, IBS, etc.).

It was a bit like wanting to be Harrods and Poundland all at the same time – saying I wanted a certain type of customer, but being happy to see any other type of customer (just in case!). I ended up falling between two stools.

It never occurred to me that I might be able to say something like, 'I help women executives who are struggling to hold down a powerful job, keep it together at home and win a losing battle with food' – which might have been a great niche, but sounded so very narrow.

And because I didn't dare do those things, I didn't attract enough of any of those groups to make a good living.

I blamed my lack of success on the psychology of the people in that group, I blamed it on the market, I blamed it on the NHS hostility to complementary therapies. I blamed it on everything but me and my confidence in myself to keep going until I got it right.

The irony was that I was doing some things right. I did manage to appear in a BBC documentary on eating disorders, I did write articles on it, I did create an online programme (which clients loved) called Ditch the Binge. It's just that I didn't know which things were working and which weren't – or why.

I did a lot of things that might have worked if only I had had the know-how (and the courage) to be bold and state in very specific terms exactly who would really benefit from my help.

What I really needed to do was clearly identify a LUCRATIVE group who WANTED my help, rather than NEEDED it.

Remember, we all spend more money on what we want (and take the steps associated with getting it) than we do on what we need.

The truth was, I feared missing out on business if I narrowed my niche any further.

I am guessing this is all too familiar for you too.

You see the wide ranging potential for the skill you have and you don't want to restrict yourself in any way, by saying you only work with specific groups of people.

The truth is, working within a narrow niche makes it infinitely easier to be successful than saying you can help anyone or everyone with a certain problem.

Saying you work with everyone doesn't make it easy for people to recommend you and it doesn't make it easy for people to understand what you do and it doesn't make you memorable.

It makes you have to work harder with your marketing – and that means more money and more time. And you want to spend less - and make more - of both.

LUCRATIVE NICHE ADVANTAGE

There are three advantages to having a clearly defined lucrative niche:

1. It allows you to stand out and that makes it easier for people to see you.

2. It helps define your brand and gives you a clear focus for all of your marketing, including choice of words and images.

3. It enables you to sell more – and/or charge more.

Your *best* niche describes your *ideal* customer or client – who is looking for just the situational-specific solution you are offering - and is willing to pay what it's worth.

If you want a serious income, you need a lucrative niche. If you want a fulfilling life and business, you need a niche you are passionate about serving.

This doesn't mean you have to give up working with people who can't afford you.

Those who say they 'can't afford you' at a new investment level are often the same people who say they 'can't afford you' at your existing pricing level.

People do not invest in what they need. They invest in what they want.

Many people will say they can't afford you when actually they can. They just choose not to. They may prefer to go on holiday, buy a widescreen TV or an iPad, for example. That is their prerogative.

As you expand your business and your income and you are able to create a place of financial security for yourself, this enables you to expand the availability of your unique expertise to more people through lower level investment products like books and cd's, apps and home study programmes, for example.

In this way, you extend your reach to many would never otherwise invest in you; and many more who will, once they know more about you and what you do

Perhaps you are highly motivated by altruism and giving back? Great. Creating a great living for yourself makes that an easier option.

Remember the oxygen mask analogy. Take care of yourself first, so you can take care of others.

When you hold yourself in a place of poverty through insisting that you are helping more people when you charge lower fees, you are living in a place of denial – that hurts you and hurts the very people you so dearly want to help.

Once you are creating the income that is possible for you when you offer longer term, high end programmes, you can choose to donate a percentage of what you make to a charity of your choice; you can invest time or money in projects or places that need altruistic entrepreneurship to survive; you can provide the benefits you want for your family, your children, your partner, your parents; but most of this only becomes possible when you are creating a sustainable income.

A lucrative niche gives you the power of choice.

LOVE YOUR CLIENTS

Please don't think all this talk of niche and lucrative niche means you give up on working with the people you love in favour of a fast buck. Quite the contrary.

I have learned that it is possible to create a great income, working within a narrow niche and still able to work with people you love to work with. How cool is that?

There is no point at all in picking a niche you don't like. Picking a niche also means having the freedom – and the confidence – to choose to work with dream clients.

This is your life and your business. You want to feel fulfilled and expanded and empowered – and you want that for your clients too, don't you?

Pick clients like you pick friends. You want to like them and want to spend time with them and share in the celebration of their successes and support them when they fall down.

Expect – and demand – nothing less of yourself.

7 STEPS TO A LUCRATIVE NICHE

STEP ONE: RE-DEFINE THE BUSINESS YOU'RE IN

Most people think of themselves, their business – and, therefore, their potential clients – in terms of the job they do. After all, the commonest question at networking and social events is, "So, what do you do?"

In order to really find your niche, you need to step out of the mind-set associated with what you call yourself – and think about what you really do.

Recognising that your expertise has wider applications can open a wider variety of dream clients and lucrative niche opportunities, way beyond what you currently believe is possible.

For example: The 'stay at home mum' who discovered she was really in the business of event management, team management and project management. Becoming an event organiser for medium sized businesses was a natural business niche for her.

Instead of doing something altogether different, what you are really doing is taking the things you do easiest and best – and doing them with, or for, a different (or more defined) group of people.

Let's use myself as an example…because I found this a difficult exercise to do; but it was liberating once I applied myself to it.

I was a clinical hypnotherapist and the natural response to 'what do you do' was to say I did hypnotherapy. However, I subsequently learned to recognise that this was the tool I used, but was not what I did.

I thought about the clients I most liked working with. I thought about the outcomes they achieved; and the way we worked together to make those outcomes possible.

I realised I was in the business of personal re-invention, of helping people gain clarity about what it was they wanted and helping them identify steps that would achieve it, of helping people tap into their unique brilliance, get better at communicating their own needs with others; of helping them advance in their careers or change career completely, of helping them improve their relationships with themselves and with others, of helping make the impossible possible and do it with ease.

In short, I am in the business of helping people to tap into their unique brilliance, to get clarity on what they want and to help them to identify steps to achieve it in their own unique way, so they can advance their careers, their lives and their businesses through personal re-invention.

Knowing this gave me the opportunity to consider any number of specific lucrative niches where my skills would be highly valued.

EXERCISE: So, WHAT DO YOU DO?

Think about your own business now – and note down what skills you use daily, that you are proficient in – and enjoy doing.

State **CORE SKILLs** (that you enjoy!) in a way that separates them from your association with a specific environment or job title: e.g. negotiating contracts where both parties feel honoured, creating systems or processes that make decision making easier, building collaborative relationships, brand reputation, list building, strengthening customer relationships, building confidence, etc..

Isolate what you do that is special - and it will be something that comes easily to you. Keep a completely open mind at this stage.

Time: Spend 30 minutes brainstorming. Rule nothing out.

Now, what business are YOU really in?
"I am in the business of

Step two: Choose a category

There are SIX key categories that, approached in the right way, will create the business income and success you deserve – and still allow you to work with dream clients you love.

So, where do you find these amazing high end clients?

Once you are clear about the niche you serve with your new found 'expert status,' that's the easy bit. Briefly, you will find them in one of the following four critical categories:

Business/Entrepreneurs/ Self-employed professionals
Self-employment and entrepreneurship is rapidly rising worldwide and entrepreneurs need a wide variety of services and products to support their business growth

Marketing/Sales
From small businesses to corporations, everyone wants help with marketing and sales to attract more clients and gain new business.

Professional/Corporate
Professionals within organisations seek out a variety of specialist services to help them advance their careers and/or the company they serve.

Health/Wellness/Beauty
everyone wants to feel better, look fabulous and be healthy – and this is a growing market - making this a potentially lucrative category to specialise in.

Healing Arts

there is a rapid increase of interest in the healing arts. People want to learn new modalities to add to their toolbox and will invest in learning healing tools & healing certifications to add to their practice.

Purpose/Career Clarity

Many people are seeking clarity and progress in their career paths, or considering launching a business and need support choosing & finding their way.

I chose the first category of entrepreneur, even though you can imagine I could have chosen any of the others just as easily.

To get the most from this exercise (© Kendall Summerhawk and revisions by Sage Lavine), I recommend you stimulate your creativity by choosing a less than obvious category first time round.

You can always change it…but you may be surprised just how many niche categories open up for you if you remain open and playful for the purpose of these exercises, and how much more is possible than you realised.

Which category do you choose?

STEP THREE: IDENTIFY POTENTIAL GROUPS

The next step is to look at potential groups of clients within your chosen lucrative category who would really benefit from – and highly value – your particular skills and services. For the time being, suspend any judgement about who your dream client group is. Keep an open mind.

Here's a reminder of what I decided that I did:

I am in the business of helping people to tap into their unique brilliance, to get clarity on what they want and to help them to identify steps to achieve it in their own unique way, so they can advance their careers, their lives and their businesses through personal re-invention.

Based on that, here's a short list of the many potential dream clients I might have chosen within the category of entrepreneurs, who would really benefit from the skills I identified:

- Women entrepreneurs
- Solopreneurs
- Health & Wellness practitioners
- Hypnotherapists
- Small business owners
- Start-up entrepreneurs
- Creative entrepreneurs
- Windfall entrepreneurs
- Reluctant entrepreneurs
- Artists & writers

When you step away from the limiting thinking that associates what groups of dream clients you can serve with the 'job title' you hold, you see how so many different opportunities open up for you in just one category. **Imagine going through this process for all the categories!**

It may seem counter intuitive, but remember: the narrower the niche, the broader the profits.

EXERCISE: LIST ALL THE SPECIFIC GROUPS OF PEOPLE WHO COULD BENEFIT FROM YOUR EXPERTISE WITHIN YOUR CHOSEN CATEGORY.

_____
_____
_____
_____
_____
_____
_____
_____
_____
_____
_____

_____

Don't decide yet if they do - or don't - need your services. First you are going to dive deeper into the problems that each of these client groups has.

Spend 15 minutes brainstorming. Rule NO-ONE out.

STEP FOUR: IDENTIFY WHAT PROBLEMS YOU ARE SOLVING

Now you see that the 'thing you do' has so many more applications than you realised – and there are many potential client groups within your chosen lucrative category, you can start getting into the detail of how you can serve each potential group within your lucrative niche category.

That means understanding what niggling problems they face, day in, day out, that prevent them from achieving all that they are capable of – and that they **will** be able to achieve once they invest in your help.

Taking time over this step is vital. It will form the basis of **all your marketing copy, programmes and offers** – so take the time to do it well and do it in detail.

Not long ago, I did some niche mentoring on behalf of a leading coach in the UK and one of her clients was a talented web expert.

I had to dissuade him from a niche he was very fixed on and thought was perfect for his service – cosmetic surgeons. He decided that, as a growing and competitive business, his ability to create a web site that could easily dominate the Google search ranking would be perfect for them.

He may well have been right.

He was a very nice, but deeply technical man who simply couldn't articulate what daily challenges a cosmetic surgeon had that would contribute to them seeking out his service.

He just didn't know them well enough – so, though his product may have been perfect for them, unless he could invest time or money in market research, client education and marketing communication, that could articulate on his behalf why his service was so much superior to any old SEO expert (of whom there are thousands), I advised that this was not the best niche for him at that time.

SITUATIONAL SPECIFIC BRAINSTORMING

To identify your dream client, you must drill deeper, get under the skin of your potential niche clients and 'live in their shoes', to see how they struggle daily with the problems that you are going to be able to help with; in a way that will create a powerful incentive for them to work with you, once you weave that understanding into your sales copy, your web copy, your talks and your 'products' and services.

Just in the way you can get under the skin of what physical or emotional symptoms your clients might experience, you want to get under the skin of what specific situations these problems cause them to struggle with; in ways that are holding them back from something they very much want to be, do or have.

This is where you need to demonstrate that you truly understand what their problems are, what they really want - and why - in a way that makes them feel like you have a window into their experience and their lives.

Work through the list of potential groups you have identified one by one, grab a big sheet of paper - and write down the answers to the following:

What is a problem they struggle with day in, day out?

To answer this successfully, imagine your client sitting in front of you telling you the minute detail of their struggles with life (people NEVER struggle with detail when it comes to describing their problems).

If I take the example of professionals trapped in high paying jobs they hate, the kind of problem they struggle with day in day out is seeing their life sucked away from them, earning plenty of money, but rarely seeing the hours between dawn and dusk or sharing time with the people they care about – and perhaps spending more and more time each day wondering if this is all there is in life.

What do they think they want instead?

The answer to this question is about the immediate solution they want.

In my example, those professionals might want a way to find more time in their day or their week to do the things they want. They might want more energy, more motivation, more peace of mind, more sleep.

What do they really want – what is their why?

This answer is about their deep seated desires – it's often the outcome they really want but don't currently believe is possible.

In my example, what they might really want is to escape, to do something with joy and meaning or creativity, to have confidence that they can survive financially, to discover there are options and life beyond the payslip, that their families will still love and support them and that they have a choice.

Complete this exercise for as many groups as possible. Stay open minded and don't make a decision or a choice just yet.

Take 60 minutes to complete a first draft.

STEP FIVE: CHOOSE YOUR IDEAL NICHE

Now it's time to choose the ideal niche that will attract a flow of your dream clients.

There are 5 key questions to ask yourself in order to answer the question, "is this the niche for me?" Go through *all* 5 questions with *every* group you have identified.

Q1 Is your niche BIG enough to be viable?

The general rule is that it must be at least 10,000 people or more. However, remember to think global, not local.

On occasions, there is an exception – when a great niche could be much smaller than 10,000. Say, for example, your niche is B list actors wanting to be A listers; or athletes competing at international level and wanting to become medal winners. The numbers would be small, but the willingness to invest would be high.

Q2 Are your ideas/services flowing upstream or downstream within the culture of your niche?

Flowing *upstream* within the culture that is already present within your niche means you are attempting to get them to change their mind-set and beliefs about your topic.

Flowing *downstream* means your ideas are ones your niche is likely to accept. Any time you are flowing upstream within your niche's culture you'll find marketing and making sales difficult, time consuming and costly.

Sometimes you might have a great idea for a product or service that you just know people need, but if you have to work hard at persuading them of that need at every turn, it is a message flowing upstream.

Warning: need is not enough.

People have to WANT what you are offering…and sometimes this can be a matter of timing. You could be ahead of the curve when it comes to recognising an opportunity.

Great marketing can sometimes be no more than great timing!

Q3 Using a scale of 0- 10 (10 = high) how important will the people within your niche rank solving this problem?

A 10 is a "must solve now" and 1 is "I can live with it for a long time, as is." This ranking must be a SIX or higher to make your niche viable for you.

Q4 Do the people within your niche have a history of investing in things similar to what you offer?

Remember that people will put up with a lot before they decide to invest in solving a problem. So, it's best to focus your business on solving a problem your clients already prioritize as important.

Q5 Do you love them?

You will be spending a lot of time with the people in your niche, which means you need to love these people and what you are doing with them.

When you have answered each of these questions in relation to each of the groups you identified within your category, those that have 5 Yes's are all potential lucrative niches.

Your only job now is to pick ONE.

If you have gone through an entire category and not found one group that fits, go back and repeat the exercise with another lucrative category. Trust me when I say that the time you spend on this one exercise will save you thousands of pounds and years of heartache and struggle, so don't be tempted to skip it or come back to it later!

STEP SIX: IDENTIFY THE TRIBE WITHIN THE NICHE

Think about the personality of the people within your niche group…the kind of people you want to work with, day in day out, the kind of people who value and respond to your unique brilliance, the kind of people you love – and who love you!

Consider their interests, their sex, their motivations and passions, their dreams and desires…and their hidden anxieties. These are the things that bind people together.

Just as importantly, choose the kind of people who will commit to make the changes you are asking them to make, who will turn up, who will pay on time, who will be respectful of your time and your money, and who will relish the opportunity you are holding for them to embrace positive change!

Avoid choosing a tribe who needs rescuing. However much you love them – and love the idea of rescuing, in the confines of the work you do, people cannot be rescued by somebody else, they can only be rescued by themselves.

However, if you notice a theme of attracting less than dream clients, treat it as a gift. It is revealing an aspect of your own unconscious behaviour patterns that is holding you back; and if you allow yourself to acknowledge it, you can do something about it.

Not convinced? Confused? Here's an example of how I've had to work on this myself:

I used to attract clients I loved for their personality; big, bold, yet vulnerable at the same time. It seemed like they would be the perfect action takers who would run with the gifts I was sharing with them; and quickly turn around their lives and their businesses.

However, I started to notice that a theme was occurring often enough for it to be more than random chance.

These same lovely people, who started with a burst of enthusiasm and made some quick gains, would then stall, stop taking the action that brought them the gains – and get sucked into some crisis or other that was, in their eyes, making it impossible for them to continue on the path of change that they had started with me.

In effect, they would drop out – and think it was ok to stop paying (because the crisis meant they couldn't any more); even though, contractually they knew they had agreed to commit to pay for a full 6 months or a year.

I would experience some uncomfortable feelings: a part of me felt like I had failed; and this led me to doubt the quality and value of my programmes, my gifts, my contribution. (Sounding familiar?)

However, these clients were actually a gift to me.

The pattern they presented me with revealed to me so many things about myself – that was feeding unconsciously into all my client relationships.

I realised I had such empathy with that dramatic way of behaving (these were the challenges which held me back for so long), that I failed to create crystal clear boundaries at the outset (with the excuse that I wanted to create a warm, relaxed environment, where we would all be chums celebrating success together).

I absolutely did want a relationship where we would celebrate success together; where I was 100% committed to them and their success.

However, unwittingly, I had also created an environment that was so relaxed, it made it seem like it was ok for someone to ignore boundaries that are vital to maintain if both client and practitioner are going to achieve the success that is possible for them.

My own coach taught me (from work with horses!) that if you act the same way three times, you have created a rule and you have trained them. I have found this to be true with people too.

I needed to learn that I could be relaxed in style with my clients, but that didn't mean relaxed around boundaries – because this created confusion for all of us; the "He said, she said, you said, I thought…" type of confusion that benefits no-one.

So, whilst you may find the concept of annual clients and contracts alien at this point – there is no doubt you are familiar with unwanted patterns of behaviour in clients; like attracting people who always want more (sessions extended, emergency calls, discounts, for example); or people who consistently fail to turn up on time, to turn up at all, to 'forget' their means of payment.

Whatever the pattern that shows up regularly, treat it as a gift that shows something you need to work on yourself.

And when you do that, you can get much clearer about who your dream clients really are – you can stop choosing clients who are never going to make the progress they should, because they just aren't committed enough, or they expect you to make the change for them.

Ask yourself how it feels to work with dream clients, including how they respect you and your boundaries around time and money.

As ever, use positive language for your answers; and express it in the present tense.

Non-Ideal use of language: "I don't want clients who expect me to be instantly available every time they think they are having a crisis."

Ideal use of language: "My clients value my expertise and my time."

STEP SEVEN: MAKE YOUR FINAL CHOICE

Use your answers from the previous exercise to complete this description of your niche.

My dream client is a *(Column A)*

_____

who struggles with *(Column B)*

_____

and wants to *(Column C)*

_____

by learning how to *(Column D)*

_____

so he/she can *(Column E)*

_____

and *(Column F)*

_____

By the way, this is only a choice for now. You are not wedded to it for the rest of your life. Try it for 3 to 6 months and see how it works for you.

If it doesn't work as well as you liked or it doesn't feel right, go back through the exercise and pick again; but don't use this as an excuse not to choose – or a reason not to give it a 100% of your effort.

Many highly successful people change niche often…it's ok to do that. The world will not stop revolving and people will not stop taking you seriously.

In fact, the moment you find the niche that is just right for you, it will be like falling in love. Everything will just start falling into place.

Chapter Eight:
Reframe 7 - Core Marketing Strategies

Meaningful marketing

When most people talk about marketing, they are really talking about promotional activities.

However, marketing pervades every part of your business and each decision you take influences what kind of customers you attract, what you can charge and what people think of you. It is a circular flow of reciprocity, with each part of your business impacting on another and influencing your success in ways you may not have appreciated fully, till now.

It lies at the heart of your business – and you need to know the impact of every seemingly small decision you take – and how it affects the healthy stream of customers, goodwill and money into your business.

Every chapter from now on is actually a marketing chapter. Each is linked like a string of DNA to the healthy functioning and success of your business; and the healthy functioning of your business means more clients benefit from the magical transformations you make possible.

One of the gifts of running your own business – outside of the constraints of any kind of institutional hierarchy, is that, instead of going with the norm, you can challenge the status quo and you can choose what to call yourself, what fees to charge, what to specialise in, how to practice and where.

Most people don't choose, though.

What you call yourself matters.

Most of you will call yourselves hypnotherapists or clinical hypnotherapists or NLP practitioners or Master NLP practitioners or something else that defines the key skill you have learned.

Those who have a vision early on of the potential and possibility to create a fulfilling and successful business might choose to call themselves something different – like a consultant or a mentor, a trainer, an author, a speaker or a founder of something, a director of something.

They are not charlatans. They are not pretending. They are setting the scene for something bigger, for business, for success.

You have the opportunity to do the same, should you choose to.

Of course, calling yourself something different and making a success of your business does require specific intent, commitment and a certain degree of fearlessness. It does mean standing out and creating a niche for yourself.

However, if you love what you do, if you refuse to give it up, if you see it as the gift to the world that it is, if you want to reach more people and make a great living, then you owe it to yourself and others to take yourself seriously enough to build a business that just might mean you call yourself something different.

Treat it as a permission slip to do different things, to branch out, to set new standards, to be innovative, creative, to make a difference – and to run a successful, sustainable hypnotherapy based business.

Avoid 'buffet' marketing

Let's say you've read to this point and decided to take action. You intend to do things differently. This time is going to be different.

However, instead of taking consistent action and following each suggested step to the letter, you treat it like a finger buffet and pick the bits you like the look of….and leave the rest, because they don't seem to fit with your version of how things work (because your circumstances are different – or so you tell yourself).

Or, you commit to do it all EXACTLY as it's suggested, but that first wave of committed enthusiasm wanes after a few weeks or months, so you start cutting corners, doing things a bit differently, dropping some of the pieces that don't seem so vital or that you find challenging in some way…..

….and surprise, surprise, you don't get the results the book says are possible.

So you go back to exactly where you started, feeling more disappointed and disillusioned than before. One step forward, two back.

Maybe it's because we live in a world where everything happens fast that we just don't wait long enough to see the fruits of our efforts; but it's a common human frailty – and one I've suffered from myself for a big part of my life.

In fact, in my case, it was such a strongly embedded pattern that I regard it as some kind of miracle that I have overcome it enough to do what I do now.

I was a really talented swimmer as a child – and tipped as someone who would be Olympic standard, but when the training got tough and my times stagnated, I gave up.

I set up in business more than once and made some successful forays, but if I got more than a couple of no's to something, I stopped asking. Each time I gave up.

I would start something with enthusiasm (anything – a life in a different country, a new home, a new job) and it wouldn't be long before I would find some reason why it wasn't working out….and would give up.

Perhaps the title of this book should be, 'Stop giving up.'

It really has been the pivotal shift for me in moving from failure to success…finally, saying to myself, "I am not giving up" and meaning it and sticking to it; and discovering, finally, that success began to happen; and, as long as I commit to not giving up, success keeps happening.

Getting clear on your dream client

If you don't know who your dream client is or what your niche is, you are shooting in the dark, and every penny you spend on marketing is scattered. The impact is diluted to the point where it is almost entirely ineffective.

When you are grateful for any client walking through your door, your dream client becomes anyone who can fog a mirror, as my coach fondly reminds me.

You know that saying, 'you can't please everyone' is true. Without effective understanding of your dream client and your niche market, you **are** trying to please everyone. It isn't possible and it can drain you of energy and life force – without building a fulfilling and successful business.

If your every moment is spent trying to find more and more ways to attract more and more people, the best you can hope for is burnout.

Spending some time to get clear on your dream client and choose a niche will save you money, time and energy. PLUS, it will build you the firm foundations of a successful business, one that will reward you one every level, financially, emotionally and spiritually.

That's worth having, isn't it?

Marketing within a niche.

Let me give you an example of how marketing within a very narrow niche works.

In the small town where I live, there is a small supermarket and around 50 yards away is a tiny shop that sells only cheese.

The cheese shop owner could figure that he is missing out on business if all he sells is cheese, because there are people who also want bread and milk and meat and vegetables. He could try to squeeze some of those things into his shop, but then there would be less room for all the cheese – and he would just be a very small shop with less to offer than the supermarket round the corner. He would soon go out of business.

Instead, he has been in the town more than 20 years, he runs a global business and ships specialist cheeses round the world. Whilst many people will buy cheese from the supermarket, those who love cheese will seek out his shop. They will choose to go there in preference to the supermarket, because he is a specialist, because he understands his market, he can talk to them about cheese, he can let them taste it. He is unique.

He knows there is a large group of people who don't just like cheese, they love it. Better still, because he is a specialist, he can charge much more for his cheese than the supermarket that is just 50 yards away. He understands that he is selling not just cheese, but an experience.

Interestingly, the same people who happily hand over money in the cheese shop go into the supermarket with a different mind-set. They may (silently) question the price of the cheese, will spend little time in the shop and may prove demanding and difficult at the checkout if there are delays (when they would happily queue in the cheese shop as they waited to get their turn).

The supermarket fulfils a basic function and plays a big number game. It can afford to be all things to all people because it can create a huge volume of customer traffic. It accepts that a different type of customer service is necessary. It must be quick and efficient.

The cheese shop feeds a passion. It cannot play a big number game. It is one man and his wife; but it can create loyalty and charge premium fees. It is special. It is exclusive. It is unique. Customer service is about taking time and knowing your customers' tastes.

I hope you see the parallels in your own business.

When you want to be all things to all people, you need to play a big numbers game – and that takes time and/or big money. When you are one person, you can play a small numbers game that commands much higher fees once you demonstrate you are unique.

USP (Unique Selling Point)

You now know a lot more about niche and you've discovered how to find your dream client is within that niche…but how can you stand out?

How can you be seen as different from everyone else in a way that helps you expand your business and attract more of the dream clients you love?

This question – and the answers to it lie at the heart of this book, at the heart of my business and at the heart of what I believe is possible for every person.

For me, it is all about reaching your potential, expanding your self-belief and discovering the pot of gold you have had hiding all along, right inside of you.

You are the answer and you are what makes you stand out.

Truly standing out occurs when you let people see who you are, when you are unafraid to be you, to express things in your way, to use your language and share your story and your perception of how the world works.

Of course this isn't an excuse to avoid listening to great advice, to avoid systems and processes and to bloody-mindedly refuse to do things differently. Neither is it a reason to stop working on your own self development.

By the same token, becoming you, fully you, means stepping into a place of confidence through revealing your vulnerability. It most certainly is not a finite place that you arrive at and get a diploma or certificate for when you log enough client hours, or attend enough workshops or supervision sessions.

It is an evolving process – and the joy is that this means your business will never stay the same, will never be quite the same as anybody else's. It will change as you change…and, because it is a reflection of you, it will remain unique as long as it is aligned with you.

When you are comfortable being you, it should show through in your web copy, your leaflets, your photos, what you say when you speak, how you dress, everything. Of course, there will be a focus to your message, but you will give yourself permission to deliver it in your own unique style…and nothing should be easier than being yourself.

Your introductory marketing message (the elevator pitch)

Imagine the scene...you are at a networking meeting and you hope to meet some people who will refer you, or work with you.

Perhaps you have already decided that this is a long slow game of building trust and rapport; so you have no real expectations of any great outcome from the first meeting.

However, irrespective of your intention, the most likely response to the question, "So, what do you do?" is, "I'm Sue, I'm a hypnotherapist."

Now, although this is a kind of cool job title and people do find it interesting enough to want to talk about it and find out more, the conversation that follows is not one that generally leads to you securing a lot of business and new clients beating a path to your door.

Instead, what follows is a conversation that is along one of three typical themes: 'look into my eyes, 1, 2, 3....back in the room,' 'can you make me cluck like a chicken'...or 'do you stop people smoking, then?' Of course there are other themes, but most of them are fed by scenes from television, film or stage.

You may go on to describe all the amazing things you can help people with...and occasionally, you might sign up a smoker or weight loss client this way; but not often.

Usually, the person you are in conversation with is fascinated but has no idea how they could possibly refer anyone to you; and that's usually because the kind of things you help people with are the kind of things your clients like to keep secret.

They are not the kind of problems (apart from smoking) that come up in casual conversation at work, in a bar or at a restaurant.

Whilst people may well ask a virtual stranger to recommend a plumber because they have a problem with a leaky tap, they will never ask a stranger to recommend a therapist because they have a problem with their digestive system or they are afraid of throwing up.

I used to spend a lot of money paying to be a member of networking groups; and a lot of time doing my best to make it easy for people to refer others to me. Whilst they loved to hear me talk, found me entertaining, and sometimes came to me themselves, they nearly all said they found it hard to find a way to easily refer me to people they met.

If only I'd known then the three secrets to getting my introduction right …and what I help my own clients with now.

- ➢ Never introduce yourself according to your job title – it may be a cool job title, but it doesn't set you apart from other hypnotherapists; and there are a lot of them about!

- ➢ Decide on your lucrative niche of dream clients.

- ➢ Get clear on what key problem you help them solve – and what outcomes are possible for them when they get that problem solved with you.

When you have those three ingredients and you condense them into a concise, attractive message – that succinctly sums up exactly what you do, who you do it for and what difference it makes to them…you have a powerful marketing message that makes it easier for people to refer others to you…even if you've only just met them.

Return on promotional investment.

Because the majority of hypnotherapists have no marketing strategy beyond, "I want more clients" – and there are few people out there to show you how to do it differently, here's some of the many tools I see them using:

- Google AdWords
- Leaflets – door step distribution
- Clinic open days
- Directory listings – on and off-line
- Search engine optimisation
- Blogging
- Writing articles for trade magazines
- Local press coverage
- Social media
- Email marketing
- Speaking

None of these is 'bad' promotional effort. However, without a strategy – which includes setting goals, getting clear on your niche, understanding your dream clients and your usp, it can be an expensive affair of hit and miss.

All good marketers use 'metrics.' In other words, they measure the effectiveness of what they do – a simple process of looking at the response rate and comparing it with the cost; so you end up with a unit cost – and an informed way of working.

You, like me, may have spent a fortune signing up for courses and products and services that are designed to improve your results – or make you an expert. Mostly, this money will never be recouped – at least not in any way you could directly attribute.

You'd think, with an MA in marketing and a whole string of jobs with marketing in the title (including Chief Marketing Officer) that I would have got this nailed quickly and easily. If you've read this far, you already know that wasn't the case.

When I was working in an hourly paid clinical practice, I spent approximately £100 – £150 per month on Google AdWords, £100 on a miscellaneous variety of other advertising, £100 a month on networking meetings and another £50 per month travelling to those meetings.

I was also spending money on supervision, CPD workshops, online marketing programmes, online hosting, online article distribution, search engine optimisation and recording and production of hypnosis CDs.

Each month I was conservatively spending £500 and more on activities (and the infrastructure) that were supposed to contribute to me getting more clients...and yet I had no real means of predicting how many clients would walk through my door on any given week.

I had no idea of my return on investment – and, if the research I've conducted with other hypnotherapists is anything to go by – neither do you.

Marketing is an art, not a science – and a technique that works brilliantly in one place can fail spectacularly in another. Without understanding the intention, the mechanics and the full 'market' picture, you are guessing and planning in the dark.

DISCOUNT PRICING STRATEGIES

Charging low to attract more clients can be counter-productive.

If you are perceived as offering a similar service to everyone else, it is true that pricing low can increase demand for your services. However, it may not be by much; and you can be setting yourself up for big problems that end up resulting in failure in the longer term.

For example, I have seen people use services like Groupon to promote their services so they can create volume awareness and effectively 'buy' a customer base.

They calculate that even though they will make very little out of the business generated directly from the offer (because services like Groupon force such a hard bargain on price), a percentage of that business will come for subsequent sessions that they can charge their normal fees for.

However, few of the people who respond to the offer are dream clients. Instead, many are 'I'll give it a try' tyre kickers, who are not massively committed to take action. They want the magic dust that you are expected to sprinkle – that enables them to make huge changes in their lives without them doing a single thing that is different.

This doesn't work of course, so not only do they not prove to be clients who come back for extra sessions (they probably baulk at the usual fees), something worse happens – that you may not be aware of.

It has been known for a long time by marketers that people share a bad experience with more people than they share a good experience. They tell the story more times and to more people. You, of course, have given the same quality of service to this group as to any of your full fee paying clients.

However, if they came with unrealistic expectations about your 'magic'– like thinking that, after one session, they would love exercise and salad instead of watching TV and eating pizza, or coming for a stop smoking session simply to appease a family member (and not because they were really ready to)…they go away with a sense that hypnotherapy doesn't work or, worse, YOUR hypnotherapy doesn't work (because they may know people who have been to other hypnotherapists with great success. Those people, of course had the right mind-set and attitude and were, no doubt, great clients.

The upshot is: this low income producing, burnout inducing period of flat out work can result in damaging your intent to create a rapid stream of referral led clients; by damaging your local reputation.

There's also the knock on effect of other local therapists potentially feeling peeved by your 'crass' promotional activity – and quietly chipping away at your reputation with their own clients.

We all make our own business choices – but it is high risk and has a sting in the tail that means you need to question whether it's worth it when it comes to selling your valuable 1:1 time.

Remember this vital rule: there is just one of you, with only so much time available – and no extra to give.

GOAL SETTING

Before you book on another CPD course to learn more about marketing, you need a simple and proven marketing plan based on a financial goal.

The idea of planning and financial goal setting my strike terror/ tedium/ panic/ avoidance into the hearts of many. I used to be the same way.

Here's how my planning and goal setting used to go:

I had a number in my head – of what I wanted to make in a year; then I'd average out how many clients I would need to see in a week to achieve that (paying little attention to the costs of overheads or what marketers call the 'cost of customer acquisition'). Then I 'hoped' that the phone would ring.

In between times I would tweak my Google AdWords, write blogs and articles related to hypnotherapy 'problems' and spend a lot of time studying ways to get more traffic to my web site, or coming up with ad hoc 'great ideas' to get more business.

That was the sum extent of my goal setting.

As you can see, planning didn't really come into it…and there was little way I could confidently measure the success of anything I was doing. It was guesswork and optimism. It was not a recipe for business success.

It seems to me that one of the biggest reasons many don't set financial goals is because they fear not meeting them; so not setting them seems means there's no risk of not meeting them. Avoidance and procrastination become the order of the day.

The only thing avoidance and procrastination guarantee is failure. If avoiding change is what we seek, then no change is what we get.

We all know that doing more of the same thing guarantees the same outcome. Yet, how easy it becomes to stick our heads in the sand and avoid looking at ourselves and our own actions in relation to our business.

If you are to stand any chance of your practice becoming a business in which you can thrive – and in which you can confidently make a great living, you simply MUST create some financial goals; and learn how to meet them.

Don't panic, you don't have to draw up a complicated grand plan. However, the basic essentials of what you absolutely MUST know – and commit to - are the following:

➢ Know how much income you want to achieve in a specific timeframe. Start with 30 days.

➢ Know who your dream client is. Then research where you can find them – online and offline.

➢ Know what niche you serve. Create web copy, articles and a 'signature talk' that speaks to that niche.

Then start taking some measureable actions that can lead you towards achieving your goal.

Measurable actions

1. Keep it simple. Do things that can be easily measured – and can create quick cash flow results. The first of those is networking and speaking.

2. Create a goal each month for how many speaking engagements you plan to have and how many networking events you plan to go to.

3. Create a goal for how many people you want to have signed up to your list and how many you want to have an enrolment conversation (initial consultation) with.

4. Create a goal for how often you will communicate with your 'audience' via email, newsletters, webinars.

5. Start measuring success rates, so you get familiar with how many talks you have to give, emails you have to send, networking events you need to go to – in order for a new client to find you and choose to work with you.

Once you start measuring, you will have information, which means you can start being more accurate in your goal setting.

You can plan how many talks to give, events to attend, emails to send, in order to get enough clients to reach the income figure that you choose.

How cool is that? You get to CHOOSE what you want to earn and you know what you need to do to achieve it!

None of it is complicated maths or metrics. It is simple estimating and testing.

There isn't room in the confines of this book to cover everything there is to know about online – or even offline – marketing; but I want you to have a broad understanding of some of the key steps you can take; why you need to take them; and how you can get started in a simple way.

Simple 7-step client attracting system

Attracting and magnetising dream clients becomes so much easier when you have a simple system for inviting them into your world. I've been hinting at it throughout the book.

I am going to share the simplest 7-step strategy for attracting dream clients to get cash and income fast. It's proven to work with all kinds of businesses, especially the solopreneur, coach and health practitioner kind of business.

And there is nothing to stop you from starting today. Minimal or no investment required.

If you have done the work in the previous chapters and are clear about your niche and your dream client; if you follow the seven steps to the letter; if you remain consistent in taking regular action; if you avoid procrastination and excuses; if you leave no step out; I guarantee it will work and your business will be transformed.

1. Create a free downloadable gift that relates to your niche and is valued by your dream clients;

2. Give this free gift away via an 'opt-in' form on your web site;

3. Create an authentic 'signature talk' in which you share your story PLUS what transformations are possible for dream clients in your niche;

4. Deliver your talk regularly – ideally twice per month.

5. Invite people to your 'list' by offering your free gift.

6. Communicate with the people on your list regularly.

7. Invite people to 'discovery sessions' or 'enrolment conversations' with you (driven by your speaking and communication with your list).

If you want to build your business fast, expand your reputation in your niche – and start getting cash in the door (without waiting several years for your referral rates to increase), you need to start implementing right away.

It is scarily simple. Not easy, but simple.

You might not want it to be the answer, preferring instead to spend more time and money on courses, services and products– patiently waiting for the phone to ring and email to drop in your inbox – from ANY client, rather than a dream client.

This is fear… and comes from a mistaken belief that you will end up being like an unwelcome caller at the front door, trying to pressure sell unwanted goods, instead of someone with a wonderful gift to share that will transform people's lives.

What it does do is put you in the driving seat. It means you are in control of your income, of how many clients you work with and of who those clients are.

LIST BUILDING AND OPT-INS

If you are unfamiliar with the term, the opt-in list is what you join every time you sign up for a free online webinar, e-book or report.

You may already have an email list which you collect to keep in touch with existing or previous clients; knowing, quite rightly, that if you stay 'top of mind' with clients, they are more likely to come back to you – or recommend you – in the future.

However, you need to create an additional opt-in list on your web site in order to start creating a relationship with people who have never met you.

Only a small percentage of the people on your list will become your clients, but the more you grow the list, the bigger the number becomes; and that means more clients in the long run.

This is about building the foundations for future business…like building a fire, it can be slow to start and does require attention to keep it burning, but the rewards are well worth it later.

To create your own opt-in list, you need two things – a downloadable 'gift' that you are willing to offer prospective clients in return for their name and email address; and an email marketing provider.

If you have been collecting your clients' emails in your sessions, but not asking permission to market to them, you will have to do so before they become addresses you can use in your email marketing.

If you don't know what an email marketing provider is – or where to find one – here are a couple you can look at to get started: MailChimp and ConstantContact. Both are simple to use and good for the beginner.

You don't have to become a technical expert, but you do need to get familiar with some of the basic marketing tools at the disposal of the solopreneur (that's YOU) even if you are going to outsource the work.

Used effectively, these tools are low cost and will play a big part in enabling you to run a business instead of spending time on an expensive hobby.

Downloadable free gift

The free gift you create needs to have relevance to your dream client – and gives people a taste of what they could experience if they choose to work with you in more depth.

It doesn't have to be lengthy, complicated or time consuming to produce.

It could be something as simple as:

5 ways, 3 tips, How to…ask for what you want in a salary negotiation/ stay calm in a business presentation/feel like you're good enough to get the man you want/sleep without pain.

The most important thing is that the title conveys something desirable and that the content is actually some use. However, a single page of A4 can be enough.

Or you could create audios of course. Ideally, though, you will want to create content that has hyperlinks and references back to your web site – or offers to take things further with you. Your consistent intent is to regularly invite people on your list into enrolment conversations.

Enrolment conversations

An enrolment conversation is similar to – but not the same as - an initial consultation.

It is a purposeful, structured information gathering exercise that helps you – and your client – fully understand what is possible for them when they work with you, and what is at stake for them if they stay where they are and do nothing.

People also call them discovery sessions or strategy sessions. They provide the ideal opportunity to invite prospective dream clients into a mutual conversation in which you both explore what's holding them back - and the possibilities that can open up for them when they say yes to working with you.

This is where you need to have an intimate understanding of the value you provide; and this is where you may uncover your own demons of self-doubt around worth.

Treat them as a gift. This is an opportunity for you to grow as a person and a practitioner – and every time that you step up to what challenges you, you provide a bigger opportunity for your clients to grow.

SIGNATURE TALK

Your signature talk is what you deliver every time you speak.

Within it, you can share great content with your audience – either a step by step high level overview of all the steps your dream client needs to take to make the change they want – or an in depth walk through of just one part.

You also want to reveal something of you, something that conveys a similar challenge you have overcome. Although you are creating a personal brand that is built on your unique individuality, your dream client also needs to feel that they know you – or they want to know more about you – in a way that demonstrates you share some common experience with them.

They need to know you understand their pain because you've shared it!

So in your signature talk, you need to share some of your commonality and your vulnerability. This is one time where you openly reveal how badly you got it wrong, screwed up, failed….as long as there is a turning point and a thing you learned that is linked to what you are able to help them with.

The most important thing to remember, though, is that making a talk that everyone enjoys is not enough.

Your talk is your business card and it needs to sell you and your programmes.

You want to walk away from every talk with a significant proportion of the people in your audience wanting to be on your list (to get your great free gift) – and a good number wanting to have a further conversation with you (an enrolment conversation).

You need to know how to make that an easy and effortless progression from hearing you talk. If you'd like more detail on how to structure your talk and what to include, you can get my free Signature Talk Template from my website at http://shirleybillson.com/downloads-from-reframe.

Decision making

Our brains are so overloaded with the demand to make all kinds of small decisions that really don't matter much (like which brand of cereal should I buy or what type of coffee do I want)….that when it comes to the big decisions, we are lost.

A simple yes or no, this niche or that niche, invest or don't invest, this course or that course, takes on such monumental proportions – that many of us, inevitably, just opt out of making the decision at all.

Sometimes, we convince ourselves it's merely a delayed decision; other times we know it's just not a decision we are ever going to make.

I've heard it said that successful people make big decisions quickly; and I am beginning to see the truth in that.

The first thing to make a positive decision on was the decision to make decisions.

So often we get ourselves caught in overwhelm by things on our list or things in our head that we haven't yet come to a decision on....and it becomes like compound interest, building stress that gets added to every day we fail to reach a decision. ("I'll do that later, I haven't time now, I don't have enough information, I don't have enough experience…").

I learned that when I make a decision in the moment…I begin to feel so much more in control of my life and my business.

When the first thought is, "I'll decide that later," make a decision about when later is. Set a time for when you will decide; and stick to it.

When your first thought is, "I don't have enough information or experience", make a decision about when you will have enough. Sometimes you don't know exactly, so decide to set a date or time to take action anyway…aware that imperfect action now is usually better than perfect action later.

As a society that rewards getting it right and punishes getting it wrong, we can become frozen in indecision for fear of making a mistake. Yet it will hold you back from the success you are capable of.

Perfectionism is a handicap in effective decision making. For business success, you need to risk getting it wrong and trust that this is ok – because you are learning.

The worst decision you can take is to stop moving forward, to stop taking action, to stop taking decisions.

Decide when, not if.

➤ Decide when you want a fulfilling and financially rewarding business.

➤ Decide when you are going to find a lucrative niche – and take steps to figure out how.

➤ Decide when you are going to increase your fees and introduce high end programmes.

➤ Decide when you are going to start working with a high end mentor or coach.

Write those down NOW as action steps to take when you put this book down.

It's easy to procrastinate, to plan something for tomorrow or next month or next year. It is easy to say or think, "I'll do that when I've done this," "I'm not ready," "Later," "When I have more time, more money…."

All of these are excuses. You might be able to satisfy your inner critic with these platitudes and 'reasons' for not getting the life and business you want…However, you need to beware any sentence that starts with "Yes, but…"

This way of thinking is what prevents action. It is so easy to do ….and takes considerable commitment to change, but change it you MUST if you are to succeed in making money doing what you love.

I have seen many people falter, not because of their lack of ability or desire…but because of their lack of awareness to see excuses for what they are.

Case Study

I had a conversation with a hard-working, dedicated client recently, who is just starting out on her business journey. I had allowed her to stretch a deadline for beginning getting into action on her business because she was adamant that she could not mentally commit to anything until she completed her coaching qualification portfolio.

We celebrated that it was complete, and she had put in some hard work around determining her niche, by working through one of my self-study programmes, Powerhouse Niche Bootcamp. I now asked her to set a financial goal.

She paused, stuttered, stumbled…started to talk about 6 months, then 12 months. I stopped her and said, "What is your goal for the next 30 days? When are you going to get your first client?"

She tried to push out the goal of getting a client by another three months, with talk of getting web sites sorted, going on another course, reading another book….yet she had been quite clear, both on this specific coaching call…and at the outset of our relationship. Making money and being a financial success doing what she loved was critical.

The question of being very specific right now – about getting a client and making some income commitments held her like a deer in the headlights…and brought her face to face with her fear and lack of belief in herself when it came to making money.

I challenged her to have either one client or £1000 within 30 days. She felt out of her comfort zone completely…but I gave her no place to hide. I knew – and so did she – that she had everything she needed (skill, ability, knowledge, desire). She just had to take action in the face of fear.

There is no person reading this who is not capable of achieving everything that is promised between the covers, if they get out of their own way.

However, if you are to break out of an old habit, an old pattern, an old way of thinking (especially one that might be shared by people in your family or your existing friendship group) that stacks up reasons, excuses and lies...you will need someone who holds you as powerful, who keeps you on the path, who challenges you when the BUTs kick in.

And you will need to agree a partnership of commitment with yourself...that says, however much I am feeling challenged, I know I have everything I need to do this; and do it.

If you are a fan of Harry Potter, you may remember a scene in one of the books, where Dumbledore tells Harry to make sure that he drinks every last drop of a magical potion, even if he begs him to stop. He urges Harry to fight every impulse to stop inflicting evident pain and distress, knowing that, they will never achieve what they need to achieve unless they are to fulfil the task. Exactly as he described, Dumbledore pleads with Harry not to make him drink any more of the potion, evidently in great pain, but because Harry loves and trusts him implicitly, he carries out Dumbledore's wishes until the last drop is drunk – at which point the magic spell is broken, the pain has gone and they have, achieved what they both set out to do.

It reminds me of some of those tough moments in making major breakthroughs in our own lives.

If you need a coach to make this happen, find one who seems to walk the talk. If they aren't charging very much, ask yourself honestly – how can they give you the confidence to charge what you're worth and step into your value if they aren't doing the same for themselves?

Chapter Nine:

Reframe 8 - Charging

Most of my clients baulk at the thought of putting up their fees.

They come up with all kinds of reasons...most commonly," no-one will pay that" and "no-one has any money."

These are capable, talented people with no shortage of clients, current or past, who think they are great.

Many say they would happily ask for higher levels of investment if they were asking on behalf of someone else – and feel ok about it; but when it comes to themselves, they are less confident.

And that's because they are afraid of being 'salesy;' or afraid that people will be offended and not like them; or that they will lose business, or that they are being greedy.

However, the kind of outcomes your dream clients get to benefit from invariably have financial and priceless life changing implications – like the confidence to go for that interview that leads to a better job, the self-worth to ask for a pay rise or set up a business, the self-belief to go out and win new business, the assertiveness to talk to the person that led to the relationship or the deal that transformed their lives – to move home, to leave home.

I remember one particular client saying to me that if he had known the outcomes that were possible for him at the beginning, he would gladly have paid me 10 x what I asked him.

He saw the value before I did.

If you accept that you are the catalyst for massive change, that without seeing you and experiencing the 'magic' that you create – your clients would never have made those monumental shifts in their lives – shifts that go way beyond the weight loss, or overcoming the panic attacks, or the insomnia, or whatever it was they initially came to you for.

When you truly own your part in those outcomes, you will see that the value of what you offer exceeds a 4 or even 5-figure investment many, many times; and because you see it, your dream clients will see it too.

The only difference between you and any high end practitioner is having the confidence to step up to that value and charge what you are truly worth; because charging what you're worth means you have to have powerful conversations around money in all kinds of situations – with clients, with suppliers, with friends and partners and family.

And powerful conversations around money evoke other fears – like not being liked, not being approved of, like standing out, like being rejected.

However, when you step up to these challenges – and embrace the courage it takes to move past them, you not only increase your income, you also become a more powerful, courageous practitioner and a more self-aware, courageous person.

Your clients get to benefit from every bit of strength and confidence you gain. You become more than a therapist. You get the opportunity, too, to become a role model for leadership and for strength.

What hotels can teach you

I used to do a popular talk to networking groups called, 'Passion, Money and Hotels,' which uses the analogy in the context of your service based business.

You know that there are hotels which charge £'000's per night and others that charge under £50.

And there are people who will pay both. In fact, people who would choose to pay £'000's would not dream of even looking at a hotel charging under £200 per night and people who choose to pay under £50 think you need your head reading if you pay £'000's.

You probably agree that it's because the quality and benefits are different….but, ask yourself this - do the cost of the benefits account fully for the whole difference – or the perceived difference?

In the hotel analogy, it is absolutely the case that some people really value a high end experience, where others just want a clean bed for the night.

What successful hotels know intimately is their ideal customer. They have no doubt where to find them, what kind of interests they have, what their values are, what matters to them and what experiences they want to have.

They understand the idea of niche and brand differentiation. They have a passion for understanding their dream clients and they know that the better they serve those dream clients, the more successful they will be, the more money they will make and the more those clients will value the experience.

You, like the hotel, have only time to sell and there is a capped limit on how much of it you have available.

What hotels understand is the power of a package or programme and how it can add real value to customers and real injections of income to their bottom line. They offer spa breaks, weekend breaks, mid-week breaks, honeymoon breaks, wedding packages, golf packages, to name a few.

Don't be fooled into thinking they are discounting their services to offer these; even though you might calculate it works out to be less expensive for you, as the customer, to buy a package than to pay the normal nightly rate plus meals.

What the hotel knows is that you may end up booking 3 nights instead of one – and, if they include one evening meal you might buy another; or, if they include complimentary wine, you may stay and eat with them instead of leaving the hotel. They know that they will actually make more money more often than had you paid the basic nightly rate.

Plus, you get a more rewarding experience – and you are more likely to come back or tell a friend – than if you only book a bed for the night. So that means they increase referrals plus the lifetime value of a customer; and their hotel has higher occupancy every night.

The more successful they become, the more people want to stay with them; and that gives them the option to increase the price of their packages, should they choose. In turn, that means they can invest more in their business and make an even more rewarding experience possible.

It's a win, win, win. Everybody benefits.

This is what you are soon to discover is possible for you.

To really charge what you're worth, you need to create programmes and packages, instead of charging by the hour.

When you learn how to create high end programmes, you can charge expert status fees that reflect the true value you bring – and you can create an environment (which doesn't have to be physical bricks and mortar) in which people don't just feel helped, they feel special and pampered and anything becomes possible; for them and for you.

Premium Pricing

I once worked with a client who never engaged fully with me or the process. I couldn't get the rapport we needed to achieve the positive change she wanted. The thing was, she told me she perceived that she was getting a less than premium product by working with me – because she bragged about the last 'top quality' hypnotherapist she had seen, who had charged her more than 3 times my fee. The thing was I knew who this therapist was, I knew her training and expertise was not better than mine. She just happened to have a clinic in Harley Street (which, incidentally, is VERY easy to get).

I never forget now that– at some level - people associate quality with price.

Most people associate quality with price

We see this played out everywhere we look. Look at luxury perfumes, skincare, high end cars and fashion (e.g., Dior, Mercedes, Mulberry, Aston Martin and the newer luxury brands like Lexus or Diesel).

Even the supermarkets aiming at a mass market adopt this strategy with their luxury and 'finest' ranges. We expect those products to be higher priced because we expect them to be higher quality; and we expect them to be higher quality because they are higher priced.

When choosing a solicitor or an accountant to handle something that you imagine has high risk and high value, the likelihood is that you will choose the professional who charges high. You will almost certainly not pick the one who charges least.

Consider private healthcare and private education. In the UK, healthcare and a good education are free, yet growing numbers of people choose to 'invest' in identical services because they expect to get greater value.

They will, of course, find some justification for those choices – like nicer rooms, higher tech equipment, more personal attention – yet, the quality of the teaching staff or the medical staff is likely to be entirely equivalent.

The thing is, the basic product is identical, but people will choose to pay extra for additional benefits that they believe make the product better.

Here's an example of a piece of psychological research – a case study from Robert Cialdini's 'Influence (source: blog.kissmetrics.com/5-psychological-studies).'

It describes how a local jeweller managed to sell out of turquoise jewellery because it was accidentally priced at **double** its initial price, instead of half.

She had intended to halve the price in order to sell off this slow selling stock. However, to her surprise, the inflated price now made the jewellery irresistible to buyers, who had previously ignored the colour over all others.

Now that the price had been raised, the context of turquoise jewellery had shifted. It now had a "high value" in the buyer's minds, even without an explanation!

In the same way, you can create a high end experience for your clients, which will allow them to fully appreciate the value of what you do – and feel good about paying more for it.

Case study: The coffee shop lesson

I have to confess I am a bit of a coffee addict and a coffee shop connoisseur. However, it wasn't that long ago, that coffee was just coffee – a commodity that was highly price sensitive. In other words, there were certain (low) price points, above which a business would lose custom.

A business just couldn't 'get away with' charging much more than anybody else; and people would reel with shock and complain loudly (to themselves and their friends, of course…I'm talking UK here!), with words like 'extortionate' and 'outrageous' liberally sprinkled throughout their sentences.

The thought of an actual coffee bar – in the UK, at least, - was something that didn't seem to be a sustainable business model; until Starbucks came along – and changed the US and UK attitudes – about what coffee was and what it was worth.

Suddenly, we were paying double and triple what we used to pay for coffee – and, though we still complain about it, it doesn't stop us wanting it; lots of it.

It isn't because we needed it. It was because we wanted it.

Not only have we have learned to love coffee in a way we never did – we actually see the commodity differently. It is no longer a basic staple item in our lives – it is a luxury and an indulgence.

Coffee now has the ability to be decadent – and very high end.

The coffee bars understood who their dream clients were and what kinds of things bothered them on a daily basis.

They took the time to realise that there were many professionals with little time on their hands to enjoy leisurely lunches or stop for breakfast.

They were always on the go, living the 'on the move' lifestyle, and they would also frown upon alcohol during a working day; but needed some way to unwind a little, to escape the stress of the day.

What they created was an ambience, a space where people could relax, chat with friends, be alone without feeling lonely, work without feeling stressed, network without feeling pressured.

Plus, they sold coffee.

They taught us to be connoisseurs about it – and offered us lots of choices, based on the same simple product; and without adding lots of extra work into the delivery of the product.

The ***Starbucks brand promise*** is *"we give you a moment in your day where you can just escape and spoil yourself."*

The lesson here is around truly understanding who your client is - and what your client wants – beyond the 'product' you think you are selling.

That means getting under the skin of their lives, understanding how they live, what pressures they have, what daily challenges they face….and how you can help make that easier.

Of course, you can offer something way better than making it easier to get through the day – or momentarily escape from it.

You can offer the possibility for making huge changes in someone's life; you can alter the entire trajectory of their future life choices in a positive way. You truly can achieve life changing results for them.

But you have to see beyond the basic commodity of 'I do hypnotherapy,' and you have to start understanding what you offer to your dream client that is special and valuable – and that they want, rather than need.

When you can effectively communicate that understanding to your prospective clients – through your signature talk, your promotional copy and your enrolment conversations, they will not choose you on price.

They will choose you on what they believe is possible for them by working with you. It is not what they need. It is what they want.

THE VALUE OF GIVING PEOPLE WHAT THEY REALLY WANT

This is where you need to do some serious personal work around 'owning' the value of what you do.

Right now, your website probably says that you help people lose weight, stop smoking, get confident, overcome phobias, etc. I could probably randomly Google any hypnotherapist site and discover the same kind of wording.

To which you might respond, "Well, that's what we treat – and that's what people want help with." Indeed.

At least, that's what we all think; and the reason we think that is because that's what clients say when they first meet us and we sit with pen poised over our client information form, asking them,

"So what did you need my help with..?" or words to that effect.

However, if the 'problem' they say they want to overcome was not causing them any great inconvenience in their lives, they probably would never seek help with it.

If I wasn't bothered, for example, by finding nice clothes in my size, or fitting in aircraft seats or worrying what people thought of me, or fearing for my life...then I wouldn't seek out a weight loss solution, because I wouldn't see it as a problem.

And if I never had to go anywhere on a plane and didn't really care for travel overseas, I wouldn't seek help for a flying phobia.

And I if I didn't have to go to interviews, speak in public or do anything else that gave me a panic attack, anxiety or IBS...and it didn't impact on my life in any significant way, I wouldn't seek help.

What I am getting at is that **people ONLY seek help for a problem WHEN that problem is stopping them from doing something they really want to do**; and this is the piece you need to be acutely aware of.

We will always be happy to pay more for getting help to achieve NEW things we really want to do (positive outcomes), rather than for fixing OLD things that are problems.

Here's a simple example. I'd feel excited spending money on a ski holiday and frustrated, reluctant or resentful spending money on a new exhaust for my car.

The outcomes that really matter, the outcomes your clients really want and the outcomes your clients will pay more for...relate to the specific things they can do as a result of working with you; and the specific impact doing those things has on their lives.

Working with you is an investment, not a cost

Let's imagine that our weight loss client, as a result of losing weight with your help, applies for a job she never would have had the courage to apply for because she never felt she had the confidence to succeed at in the interview – and she gets it.

Let's also imagine that this new job is paying £3000 more than the job she was in…and, because she feels so much more confident (all stemming from her work with you), she excels in that and moves on to another promotion within another 2 years (paying another £6,000, say).

This would mean that, in those 3 years since working with you – and as a direct result of the work you did together, she had earned an additional £12,000 she NEVER would have earned if she had stayed feeling fat and lacking in confidence.

You just gave her what she really wanted – a life with better opportunities, more freedom and more money. Maybe you also gave her a better relationship, a better sex life, a better social life.

The thing was - that better life wasn't something she believed was possible until after she came to see you.

You are the catalyst, the facilitator and the enabler for monumental life shifts.

Could you foresee the exact way it would work out? No.

Could you promise that every person who came to see you would make an extra £12,000? No (although some will make much more!).

Does this mean you can't tell people that this is the kind of outcome that is possible for them? NO.

In all honesty, when you help people see what is possible for them when they decide to work with you, when they take responsibility for themselves, when they take different actions – you are helping them take the first step towards making it real; and that is a powerful gift with great value.

When you start doing more powerful pre-framing work with your client – to help her see what is really possible when she works with you; you increase the likelihood of her achieving it; as you build reframe upon reframe.

Can you guarantee that she will lose a stone? No, but you can guarantee that if she commits to herself first, you will do everything in your power to help her – and she will be far more likely to lose that stone, get the promotion, or the new clients, or the new relationship; for the exact same reason.

When she first comes to see you, deep down, these are the big things in life that your client truly wants – the relationship, the great job, the income – but she daren't admit that, to either herself or you, to begin with. They seem like unachievable pipe dreams.

But it *is* what she wants…because the things that really bother her are not being confident enough to speak up in meetings, not applying for the bigger job, not asking for the higher salary if she does get offered the job, not setting up in her own business, not going to networking meetings or reaching out to new clients for fear she will fail the 'opinion formed in 3 seconds test'.

Telling someone you will help them be more confident and believe in themselves isn't enough. You have to spell out exactly what is possible when they have that increased self-belief and confidence.

You know from the evidence of your dream clients that 'wished for' outcomes , like renewed relationships, promotions they never would have had, new jobs they love, new businesses; and positive new life directions all began because of the moment they decided to see you – and to commit to work with you.

The outcomes cascade and spill out from the simple results your client expects into the wider context of health and wellness, finances, family, relationships and future potential.

It all started with you. They know it started with you. It is time for you to know it too; to accept it; to embrace it; to own it; and to share it.

In other words, you have to deal with your own confidence and belief issues first.

EXAMPLE: A SLOOOOW LEARNER

Let me give you an example of how I began to realise this (but resisted for several years).

Before I became a full time hypnotherapist, like many of you, I had a job and did my hypnotherapy in the evenings and at weekends.

One evening, a group of contractors, who worked in the NHS trust I was employed by as a senior manager, organised a small social gathering to which I was invited. I sat next to a guy I had had limited professional dealings with and, naturally, we got into a conversation where he asked about my hypnotherapy (you know how excited you get to talk about the thing you love!); and I asked about his life and family.

He was from Northern Ireland and was commuting to England every Sunday night and not returning home to Belfast till late Friday. He told me how he missed his family, how he would dearly love to spend more time with them, with his friends – and do more of the things he used to love – that would also help him keep fit and lose weight, but now couldn't commit to because he could never get to training or make any guarantees about his weekends.

He was at the beck and call of his work – and resigned to it.

I honestly don't remember the exact things I said to him…but, as a solution focused hypnotherapist, I am sure I naturally asked him questions that helped him access his own resources, with a little intuitive re-framing thrown in for good measure. We said goodbye and that was that – a pleasant evening spent with pleasant people.

Not long after that meeting, I handed in my notice at work, so that I could become a full time hypnotherapist; following my heart and my passion.

Almost exactly a year later, I received an email from this same guy which astonished me.

With his permission, I share it here:

Hi Shirley,
I am just writing to let you know that you started a series of events by telling me to 'just do it'.
I am now back in Belfast working in partnership with a great guy called ………..
Since February we have been helping companies and organisations get through the current down turn.
I am home with my family, taking an active role and also losing weight nearly 20kg since February.

Keep in touch.

Regards

Ivan Roche

This was fabulous to receive but it got me curious about how he could possibly attribute all of this change to me.

Despite feeling a fraud by asking, I asked if he would allow me to share his feedback as a testimonial on LinkedIn – as I had heard that online testimonials were vital to have.

All my other testimonials were on handwritten notes or texts – and I didn't like to go back to clients and ask for additional praise. Can you hear the childhood echoes of 'no-one likes a show off?'

This is what he wrote (no, I didn't write it for him and no, I haven't edited it at all).

Shirley is one of the few people that I have met in my life that has the personality to put you immediately at ease. Having put you at ease she has an incredible ability to get you to focus on the key issues and more importantly to make a decision and move forward. As a result of working with Shirley I have changed my life and have spent more time in the last year with my loved ones then I did in the last six years. I would recommend Shirley to anyone who is prepared to listen.

Whilst this was lovely to read, the person who had most trouble believing in it was me. I genuinely could not see how I could honestly take any credit for what he was giving me credit for – when all we had shared was a pleasant evening of conversation.

You might be thinking the same….it isn't right to take any credit. After all, even if he had been a fully-fledged paying client, I would still be saying – rightly – that, any change is down to the client. We, after all, are only the catalysts for change. Without client commitment, nothing changes.

All true.

However, here's the learning that it took me another 4 years to figure out…

… I began to realise it was important for me to take the credit –not for guaranteeing any of those things – but for honestly holding those amazing changes out there as possible for my dream clients.

And the dream client is the key part of that. You know, as well as I do, that the people who make those massive shifts **are** your dream clients. The trick, therefore, is to get better at identifying them – and finding more of them; but first you have to own up to your part in their change; and then assign a value to it.

Managing resistance

Whilst, in theory, it is a simple reframe to go from 'cost of a treatment' to 'investment in potential outcomes' – for many, this simple reframe encounters huge resistance and requires a massive mental mind shift.

It did for me.

Who better, though, to take on the notion that such shifts are possible than you?

After all, it's what you work on with your clients, day in, day out. Isn't it time to start working on you?

When you recognise that beliefs around money, value and worth are just as rooted in trauma, drama and 'fiction' than any other fear, phobia, anxiety or mentally-induced condition that your clients bring you, you can begin to change them.

Just as with your clients though, you have to choose to change it – and commit to do the work to change it.

The catalyst could be this book, but the work is up to you.

As a solution focused practitioner, I was trained to keep the client forward-facing, so they could access the positive, left frontal lobe of the brain and move out of the negative spiral of thinking that was keeping them stuck. I still practise that.

However, it sometimes pays – when it comes to helping clients (and helping yourself) to make big life shifts that feel challenging and uphill at times - to remind them/you of the real costs of not taking action and not making changes.

The motivation to move forward is driven by the need to get away from the past and the fears that have held us back, yet when we get tired, when we start to doubt the light at the end of the tunnel (our desired outcome) is really there, is really possible to reach, is really able to deliver the outcome we want;, then we can falter and stop – and go back to the very thing we were running from.

That is when you - and your clients – need reminding of the cost of NOT taking action; to reconnect with the motivation and the desire to get what is possible, if only we keep taking the steps.

EXERCISE: The value of working with you

Draw a circle and, in it, write down the basic outcome a client could have achieved from working with you. E.g. lose 10lbs. Then draw 4 concentric circles around the first and label each one:

I. Health

II. Social/family

III. Finances

IV. Future potential

Within each of the concentric circles, brainstorm the potential secondary and primary results your clients get as a result of achieving the basic outcome.

The more you can relate the results your clients get to EVERY aspect of their lives, the more you'll be able to charge.

The cost of not working with you

Repeat the exercise, above…this time assessing the negative impact on each area of your prospective client's life if they DON'T take action to change it.

You will be amazed how different you feel regarding the impact of your work – and the true value of it!

Charging what you're worth attracts more of your dream clients

Let's consider dream clients.

Dream clients turn up on time. Dream clients turn up for all their sessions – unless something really unavoidable stops them; and, even then, they let you know. Dream clients do the work. Dream clients are committed. Dream clients get results. Dream clients give you testimonials. Dream clients refer you.

Less than dream clients think it's ok to turn up late, to not turn up at all, to not pay, to not do the work, to cancel you, to question the value of what you do, to tell you you're too expensive and that they can't afford you, to tell you 'it' doesn't work.

Charging what you are worth (which is way more than you are currently charging) makes people stop and think. It makes them consider how much they want something, how important it is to them and it makes it more likely that they will commit to take action in a much bigger way – than if it cost no more than an evening for two at the cinema.

The truth is that money – and charging what you are worth - makes people think. It makes people, rightly, question value.

I have known clients I might assume to have very little means to invest, see the astonishing life changing potential and value of what they are investing in, so they commit – and they get results.

I have also known people who, outwardly, appear to have great resources to draw on, yet choose not to invest in their own future.

So, when someone tells you that the thing they want help with is the most important thing in their life, but reject it in favour of an iPad, or an iPhone, or cosmetic surgery, or something else, you know they don't truly love themselves enough yet to make themselves a priority.

This is not a judgement of people or class. It is a judgement of commitment; and a judgement borne out of a deep desire for people to love themselves enough to commit to their own welfare, their own wellbeing, their own future, their own success.

It is what I call 'loving yourself rich.' To get the riches we deserve – whether it be health and wellbeing, financial prosperity, relationships or a dream fulfilled – we must love ourselves enough to commit, to invest and to do the work that will result in the change that we want.

OPEN THE DOOR TO BIGGER INCOME OPPORTUNITIES

When you charge what you are worth, it also means stepping into a new environment of like-minded practitioners, who also charge what they are worth – and that can open doors to opportunity that you will never otherwise see.

Practitioners who charge what they are worth recognise that they are running a business. They remain authentic, adhere to the standards and ethics of their professional bodies and work with integrity – and they understand that they help fewer people by behaving as if their chosen profession were a hobby.

One of the many things they do is collaborate and work in partnerships or joint ventures. They know that this expands their business and income potential and can add value to their own clients.

They are ever alert to new people who, perhaps, have expertise in a field of knowledge or practice they do not, for example. That person might be you.

For example, since working on high end programmes with high end clients, I have been invited to speak at events I would never have imagined were possible for me before.

However, if you charge a low hourly fee, with no 'high end' packages or programmes, it makes it highly unlikely that you will ever be invited to collaborate on any level.

You may mistakenly think there is some kind of charmed circle of people with more expertise or knowledge than you. This is not the case. They are simply mindful of the value of what they do – and they charge accordingly.

Attract High End Clients with High End Programmes

If you are to create a 'safe' and sustainable income, it is not just possible, but desirable, to offer high end programmes – and to do it straightaway.

You do not have to wait until you think you have enough experience or wait until you have enough clients or wait until you are already achieving a certain level of success. You can start right now. Today.

Once you start working with high end clients, you will create the same level of income from working with just a few that you would normally need to work with hundreds to achieve.

And that creates a platform of security, which flows into the energy you take into every client relationship – which means you are at your absolute best with every one; plus, it frees up time and energy to create group programmes as you build your business – and that means you get to serve more people at lower price points, without risking your income and your health.

Win, win, win, win.

Of course, unless you are someone who is already in one of my own high end programmes, you may not believe this; so let's go exploring.

Who is a high end client?

I used to associate the term 'high end client' with celebrities, aristocrats and high earning executives. It seemed to me that the only way I could increase my hourly paid income would be to find a way to create a client base within one of these sectors – and, as someone who grew up in a small semi-detached house in the London suburbs – I didn't know many of these.

I contemplated a Harley Street practice – and have seen many do the same; but part of my work life strategy was to work how I wanted to work – without the commute, the city drama, the travelling expense.

Had I lived in London, I might have chosen differently, but I'm glad I didn't; because it made me keep searching, keep testing, keep looking for a way to create a fulfilling, sustainable business **on my terms.** I'd walked away from the city life and the pressures that go with it. I wasn't prepared to go back.

A high end client can be someone just like you or me. They don't necessarily live in a big house, drive an expensive car or have a huge income. Quite often the opposite is true.

A high end client is someone who is looking for answers to a problem they can't solve – and is willing to invest a significant amount to get the solution – once they understand the true cost of the problem and the true value of the solution.

And this is where you come in. Y*our* high end clients are looking for answers to a problem *you* know how to solve – and you know how to help them see what is possible for them once they have solved it; and take the steps to get there.

High end clients often appreciate you more and demonstrate that appreciation with glowing testimonials. Plus they are often more committed to do the work required to get the outcomes they want.

This results in your reputation growing stronger and faster.

This gives you increased confidence. This feeds back into your client work.

Clients get even better results because of it…and you get even more glowing testimonials…and the cycle continues.

What is a high end programme?

A high end programme is a way for you to offer – and for prospective clients to benefit – from the very special and unique expertise you now realise you have; for you to charge what you are worth – and for them to understand and fully appreciate that value.

Private High End Programmes REPLACE your regular therapy sessions!

Recognising and acknowledging your personal brand magic is the starting point for understanding how it is possible for you to create high end programmes and charge what you are worth – which is truly 10 times or more what you currently charge.

Here's the really beautiful part.

The content of a high end programme will not involve you in a huge amount of extra work. It just requires you do the following:

Take stock of all the things you currently do and provide for your clients, like free hypnosis audios, recordings of sessions, helpful reference materials and/or checklists, emergency telephone calls. There is always much more than you currently take account of.

Discover what your 'signature system' is. This is simply a way of unlocking your unique expertise around how you do things–which is much more systematic than you realise. You'd also be amazed at how much of your personality and previous experience comes into your work with clients – and can add value in ways you aren't currently aware of. Your signature system transforms 'that thing you do' into a step by step system that tells clients exactly what they get when they hire you. Even when you think you have no system and that every client is bespoke, you will find there is more of a step by step approach than you realise.

EXERCISE: Creating a programme

Create an exhaustive list of EVERYTHING you do with, create for, or give to your clients, whether you currently charge for it or not.

Add anything you could possibly do/provide that you don't currently, but would be easy or fun to do/provide:

Example:

- Hour long therapy sessions
- 15 minute emergency calls
- Checklists of useful books or articles
- Exercises to do
- Pre-recorded audios
- Bespoke session audios

- ➤ Initial consultation
- ➤ Email support
- ➤ Review sessions/calls
- ➤ Coaching/counselling support
- ➤ Action plans

Put each item listed on to a single post-it note so you can play with ideas for what to include in your programmes – as core and as bonuses, using a 3 programme template (e.g., Basic, VIP, Platinum).

If you are just starting out, it is tempting to offer a basic programme first and higher programmes as you gain experience and confidence.

However, in order to generate sufficient income to give you confidence in your business, start with the HIGHER levels of programme (VIP and Platinum) and use this 3 step process to decide what to include at each level. Your basic programme will become a home study course or workshop, for example – something that you can provide one to many; or as self study.

Extract the items on your list and start adding them to each of your columns. Your middle column (VIP) might include everything in basic plus something involving personal access to you and your third column (Platinum) might include everything in your VIP programme plus even more access to you.

REMEMBER: The higher the level of the programme, the more there is ACCESS to you.

Creating BONUSES: Bonuses are EASY and require NO EXTRA WORK. Simply decide what is to go in each programme, add a £VALUE to each one – then decide which will be described as bonuses. You do not have to create anything new.

EXERCISE: Capture your signature system

- Imagine your dream client is standing around 12 feet in front of you, having achieved everything they wanted and everything that was possible as a result of working with you. You see them smiling and grateful.

- Where you are standing is the start point that precedes their very first session with you.

- As you step forward, imagine this: what is the first thing you need to do with them, or get them to do, before you – and they - will be able to move forward to the next step?

- Record this on audio or scraps of paper; and place them in order on the floor or on a wall, so that you can move them around if necessary.

- When you think you are done with step one, physically step forward again to step two.

- Repeat the process until you reach the point where your dream client is standing and, together, you have gone through all the steps that took her here.

- If you get to a step and realise that you have missed something, go back and revise.

- Check you are happy with all the steps and the order they happen. Now you have a signature system and you can give your system a name.

EXAMPLE: MY 5-STEP SIGNATURE SYSTEM:

"How to Stop Playing Small and Love Yourself Rich" Signature System

1. **Say Yes to Possibility** - the mind-set that brought you to this point isn't what will take you to your next level. Which is why it's critical to unlock hidden skills and learn uniquely personal strategies for bridging the gap between your vision of what's possible - and where you are now, so you can take action to achieve it. This includes overcoming limiting beliefs that are holding you back and transforming your relationship with money.

2. **Say Yes to Your Unique Brilliance. Be YOU** - magically capture the spirit, personality and passion of you and what you do and the unique way you do it, giving you freedom and permission to integrate your authentic personality into your marketing. Discover how to be a success being you.

3. **Say Yes to Expert Status** – discovering how you really are an expert with unique skills means you can start defining a lucrative niche, in which people will pay you handsomely for your personal brand of magic.

4. **Say Yes to Dream Clients** - attracting dream clients means being very clear about your niche, and using a magnetising simple-to-implement system for welcoming them into your world with ease, so you become a powerfully magnetic draw for them.

5. **Say Yes to Big Income** - when you discover your own unique signature system and create compelling high end programmes, it makes it easy for clients to say yes to high end investment that reflects the true value you bring.

HOW TO GO FROM 'WHAT IS A HIGH END PROGRAMME?' TO OFFERING ONE (Summerhawk)

Right before I offered my first high end programme, I had just invested a five figure sum in my first high-end mentor and I needed to make some serious money fast.

I had only seen one high end programme before (the one I was on), so had little to model and I doubted that I could offer what I did outside of the normal hourly paid model, which meant I had a lot of questions:

- ➢ Will people really pay ME that much?

- ➢ Will people get enough value and transformation?

- ➢ Will I really be able to deliver?

- ➢ Can I really do this?

- ➢ Am I really going to do this?

The first thing I did was make a DECISION… because no action starts without a decision. I adopted a 'High End STATE OF MIND' by 'acting as if' and I trusted my MENTOR even when I doubted myself….in fact, especially when I doubted myself.

Here's what I discovered, that is the theme running through this book:

- ➢ People will invest in a High End Programme with you, even if you are newly qualified.

- ➢ You are WORTH more than you realise!

- ➢ The expertise you take for granted is PRICELESS for your clients

- People want your expertise, attention and support focused on THEM

- People want and need to feel fully committed to make BIG CHANGES - and making a higher investment focuses their attention on doing that.

- EVERY business has the opportunity to offer a high end level of service

- Statistically, approximately 20% of your EXISTING clients will happily invest in a High End Service.

- The RESULTS clients get from their transformation are worth many times MORE than what they are investing with you.

- People aren't investing in you; they are investing in themselves.

I quickly learned that the best way to attract ideal high end clients was to become a participant in a high level programme with a mentor I admired, to participate actively in that programme, take responsibility for my results, to be visible and trade in excuses for taking action.

How to create your own high end programme

The mistake I see many practitioners make is thinking something is a programme when they are actually offering a series of sessions – 6 sessions, 10 sessions, or more for example.

This is evidence that you are still adopting a 'charge by the hour' mind-set.

A programme, by contrast, relates to an outcome and has some definable content – even though you will, naturally, include therapy sessions within that.

High end programmes usually start at 3 months. Many (mine included) are 6 months or 1 year in duration.

Here's an idea of how you can create your own and what to include:

Hypnotherapy – Less is more! You can offer a specified number of sessions per month or a 'bank' of sessions that are scheduled throughout the programme period.

- Private coaching/therapy
- Q&A calls
- Short, emergency calls
- FB groups/Google groups

Momentum – Get your clients started generating results immediately and design ways to re-invigorate them throughout the programme period.

- Initial VIP day (live or virtual)
- Private topic-specific strategy or kick start call
- Group retreats
- Contests

Content – Clients love topic-specific training so look for easy ways you can deliver your expertise.

- Topic specific group or pre-recorded training calls
- Done-for-You forms, templates, checklists, scripts, etc.
- Examples of written or recorded materials you've used to achieve results

- Teleseminar programmes

Special Star Treatment – your High End clients should feel special and valued.

- Priority consideration for other offers
- Special savings on future programmes
- Goody bag at VIP days or events
- Magazine subscriptions
- Books sent quarterly
- Special seating and special dinner/breakfast at your events
- Free or lower cost tickets to your events
- Attendance by a spouse, partner or key employee at retreats or events

Bonuses – Bonuses add significant value to your programme and inspire people to say 'Yes!' to your offer.

- Topic-specific virtual intensives
- Downloadable content, e.g. expert interviews or hypnosis audio
- Full pay bonuses can include topic-specific teleseminar training
- Examples of written materials you've used to achieve results
- Fast action bonuses can include a private kick-start coaching call with you.

The 3 Most Common Mistakes to Avoid

Common Mistake #1

Making your High End programme look too much like regular therapy, coaching or consultancy.

The solution is to:

Focus on and emphasise the RESULTS (purpose) of the programme rather than on the coaching/therapy/process that gets the results.

Stop including private therapy or coaching in your lower level programmes.

Common Mistake #2

Putting too much into your High End Programme.

The solution is to:

Remember that high end clients want access more than they want quantity.

Remember that if you already have programmes, you've probably been giving away too much in them, making this the perfect opportunity to streamline your programmes and your business.

Common Mistake #3

Giving people what you think they need versus what they want.

The solution is to:

Listen to the problems and challenges your clients are telling you they are struggling with.

Listen to what areas they keep asking for help with.

HIGH END PROGRAMME SAMPLE BLUEPRINT

Coaching/therapy

- Two 30 minute monthly calls
- Three 15 minute emergency calls
- Q&A via email access

Momentum

Initial VIP day (live or virtual)

Content

- Access to pre-recorded training calls (even 1-3 calls works to get started)
- Hypnotherapy audio download
- Done-for-You forms, templates, checklists, scripts, exercises, etc.

Recognition and Visibility

Article about your client in your e-zine/newsletter.

Special Star Treatment

Special savings on future programmes

Priority consideration for your other offers

Bonuses

- 1 Topic specific virtual intensive
- Full pay bonus is topic specific teleseminar training
- Fast action bonus is private kick start coaching call

SAMPLE HIGH END SUCCESS PLAN

Target number of clients: 5 Private High End Clients

Duration: 6 months

Topic: Building Their Ideal Career

Title: Platinum Inner Circle

Problem it solves: (Be specific and tangible)

- Specific plan for how to get on 3 shortlists in 30 days
- Easy strategies to begin growing a contact list
- Help getting out of overwhelm
- How to feel confident and on track
- How to be negotiate a better salary

Cost to Client of Not Solving this Problem:

- Stress and not able to easily pay the bills
- Feeling undervalued and stuck
- Being paid less than they are worth
- Others promoted ahead of them

Programme format:

- Two 30-minute monthly calls
- Three 15 minute emergency coaching calls
- Q&A email access
- Initial virtual VIP day
- 1 pre-recorded training call
- Templates, checklists, scripts, etc.
- Interview skill audio interview
- Special savings on upcoming training
- Book sent quarterly

Bonuses:

- 1 Topic specific virtual intensive
- Full pay bonus is topic-specific teleseminar training
- Fast action bonus is private kick start call.

Full pay:

£5500

Payment plan:

£6500

Details: £1500 deposit and 5 payments of £1000

Fast action Savings:

£1000

Details: Applied if making a decision within 24 hours

Total Anticipated Revenue:

5 clients at full pay, quick decision = £22,500

Chapter Ten:
Reframe 9 – Present State of Mind

As promised at the outset, this book reveals every step to transform your hourly charging, hypnotherapy practice into a high end business. I have left nothing out and if you follow these steps, you will have all that you need.in terms of know-how to make an astonishing difference.

I sincerely hope that many more people will be helped by this book than I could ever hope to reach in person (however little I might charge for my time).

From page one, you have learned how to establish the right mind-set, how to transform your vision to goals, how to find your lucrative niche, how to price and design packages and programmes and how to attract and find new clients.

I've included many exercises between the covers of the book itself – and added more that you can download from the web.

However, we all know that knowing how to do something is only part of the picture. We wouldn't be hypnotherapists if we didn't fully appreciate the power of the mind to do one of two things – propel us forward; or hold us back.

If you are nervous about investing fully in a coach or mentor right now, my recommendation is that you work through each of the exercises on your own. Set aside time to complete them and take your business as far as you can go simply by applying the techniques and strategies within the book, one by one.

As you do so, you will discover where your own personal challenges lie and will learn much about yourself and your relationships with money, with your family, your colleagues and your friends.

At that point, I urge you to seek out a high end mentor of your own and avoid the temptation to work with a coach or mentor who is charging by the hour or charging low fees – despite the temptation.

The truth is, this would be a little like seeking guidance on prayer from an atheist. Whilst they can be talented, smart and highly recommended by others… if their own business model suggests they lack the confidence, belief or know-how to create their own high end business…ask yourself how will they help you move forward with yours?

Considering a coach and mentor

When it comes to making a big change in your business, I have learned the hard (and expensive) way that investing in high level business coaching and mentoring was not just necessary for me, but essential.

I know now that, had I invested sooner, the extra income I could have made would have more than paid for the coaching.

The first time I had a conversation with the person who is now my coach and mentor, I uttered the immortal phrases, "I'm not ready" and "I can't afford it" and put the phone down, wishing there was some way I could miraculously find the $10,000 it was going to cost.

I realise now that my question should not have been…."how can I afford it?" but "how can I afford not to?"

I laboured on under the delusion that I couldn't afford it and that if I just delayed long enough some miracle might occur that would mean I could afford it after all.

Of course, just as a miracle hadn't solved the problem before the call (which was why I was making the call), a miracle didn't solve the problem after the call.

However, I did one thing that was different (and it only takes ONE thing). I wrote down a set of goals for the year – and working with that coach in her high level programme was one of them.

I had no idea how, but I wanted it to be so.

6 months later, I had even less money than when I first made the call – but my mind-set had shifted.

I knew that, though I was scared, I was capable and willing – and if someone would show me how, I would do everything they told me to achieve the success I knew I was capable of achieving.

I borrowed, sold, racked up credit card debt – and made a solid commitment to myself. I invested in a high end coach and mentor.

It was tough and took me so far out of my comfort zone, I was often tempted to retreat to what I knew best – but I was in so deep financially, I had no choice but to keep moving forward and to reframe my perspective, repeatedly, of what was possible for me, my family, my business and for my clients.

Whether you choose to invest in a coach or mentor yourself, this book is intended to reframe your own perspective of what is possible for you and for your clients.

It is not about exploring every possible avenue for income generation. It is about how to convert an hourly paid practice that is risking your livelihood and/or your health into a business that enables you to create a platform for bigger success.

When you charge less than you are worth, you are not in control of your income or the kind of people who walk through your door; and you limit how many people will benefit from your brilliance.

I wish better for you.

If you'd like to explore the options for coaching and mentoring with me, visit shirleybillson.com/apply for more information.

Success Reframe Private Programmes, Mastermind Groups and Workshops

Success Reframe private programmes, Mastermind Groups and Workshops are for people just like you – people seeking to increase their expertise, reach more people and make a real difference in their own lives as well as in the lives of their clients.

All programmes are unique and provide a level of access to Shirley's teaching and expertise to suit everyone. Whether you want private, one to one and intensive mentoring with Shirley; the support and unrivalled motivation of a business Mastermind group; or whether you want to increase your practitioner skill set, there is something for you.

The opportunity for a breakthrough in your business and personal life is profound.

Success Reframe programmes, mastermind groups and workshops focus on a number of key business, hypnotherapy and personal development areas, including, but not limited to:

- 'Freestyle Scripting' workshops
- 'Ditch the Binge' practitioner training
- Success Reframe Private Mentoring Programme
- 'Project 6 Figure' Mastermind Group
- Private 1: 1 half day intensives
- Private 6 month and 12 month programmes
- Group Masterminds
- Training Workshops
- Skills Certification Programmes

Private mentoring and mastermind groups are available worldwide. Bespoke corporate or hypnotherapy training school programmes are possible on request.

Visit www.successreframe.com to keep updated with events, workshops and programmes.

ABOUT THE AUTHOR

Shirley Billson is an entrepreneur, author, mentor, trainer, coach and solution focused hypnotherapist. She has an MA in marketing and has been a director of 4 companies.

She has appeared on BBC TV, is an inspirational speaker and has spoken on a variety of platforms, including European and UK conferences, international business networking groups, solution focused hypnotherapy & clinical psychology training workshops and blog radio.

She is passionate about helping entrepreneurial hypnotherapists, healers and executives trapped in well-paying jobs they hate, to tap into their unique brilliance, to get clarity on what they want and to help them to identify steps to achieve it in their own unique way, so they can advance their careers, their lives and their businesses through personal re-invention.

Inspired by Shirley's calm confidence, you refresh your own instinctive decision making and are gently guided to a new place of freedom and control; which is not to say, she doesn't also employ some powerfully structured toolsets to help you make change happen on your terms – when the timing is right.

Privately, Shirley adores Spain and all things Spanish and plans to run combined boutique style retreats there as soon as a suitable venue, combining luxury and tranquillity, appears!

She has a black belt in Tae Kwon Do, loves clothes and shoes…and won't say no to a glass of Cava or Champagne when she isn't working!

You can find out more about Shirley and some of her work by visiting shirleybillson.com or allinthemind.me.uk

facebook.com/shirleybillson

twitter.com/shirleybillson

http://www.linkedin.com/in/shirleybillson

THE LAST WORD.

"I think it's fantastic. Well-written, comprehensive, strong and deep. You are so generous with all this information and you definitely emerge as not only an expert but a MENTOR that someone will be very fortunate to have holding their hand, cheerleading them and teaching them amazing skills that will help them live their dreams and affect others positively." Julie Flanders, Achievement Expert

"It is very insightful giving a lot of practical advice. What I particularly liked was including your own personal experiences and how you overcame them. I will be totally rethinking my approach to my business plan using these inspirational steps" Sherry Tolson, BSc (Hons), Hypnotherapist, Expertise Weight Management

"I just couldn't put it down. I was emotional at the end of it. I loved it and want to read it all over again! It is one of the most honest, heartfelt books I've read that really spoke to me, hit me between the eyes and made me wake up to what is possible for me and my clients. I felt as if you were sat opposite me talking to me as a friend, giving me good advice and a steer, that you genuinely care about me, my life and my clients. I just loved the explanation of what happens to - and for - all when you charge what you are worth ... the step by step sequences ... it opened a door for me, I could finally see it ... it was one that I've been trying to find for some time. I loved hearing about your experiences which completely resonated with me! Please write another one! Please let me review it!" Kim Dyke, Solution Focused Clinical Hypnotherapist and Supervisor

"I highly recommend Shirley Billson's book Success Reframe. It's easy to read and more importantly, easy to put into practice. We all want to put our creative ideas to good use and we all want to be a success. This book will help you reach your dreams." Dr. Steve G. Jones, Clinical Hypnotherapist

BIBLIOGRAPHY

Jeffers, S. (1987). *Feel the fear and do it anyway.* Nightingale-Conant.

Pagan, E. (n.d.). *Niche Intelligence Report.*

Summerhawk, K. (2013). *How to Design, Market and Fill Lucrative High-End "Platinum Sytle" Programs.* International Association of Women in Coaching.

Summerhawk, K. (2013). Brainstorming out of the box. *Niche Breakthrough Secrets.* International Association of Women in Coaching.

Williamson, M. (1992). *A Return to Love.* Harper Collins.

www.ingramcontent.com/pod-product-compliance
Lightning Source LLC
Chambersburg PA
CBHW051651170526
45167CB00001B/426